The Cotton and Textile Industry: Innovation and Maturity

This shortform book presents key peer-reviewed research on industrial history. In selecting and contextualising this volume, the editors address how the field of textile history has evolved.

Themes covered include entrepreneurial, technological and labour history, whilst the book highlights the strategic and social consequences of innovations in the history of this key UK sector.

Of interest to business and economic historians, this shortform book also provides analysis and illustrative case studies that will be valuable reading across the social sciences.

John F. Wilson is Pro Vice-Chancellor (Business and Law) at Northumbria University at Newcastle, UK. He was the founding editor of the *Journal of Industrial History.*

Steven Toms is Professor of Accounting at the University of Leeds, UK.

Nicholas D. Wong is Vice-Chancellor's Senior Research Fellow at Newcastle Business School, Northumbria University, UK.

Routledge Focus on Industrial History
Series Editors: John F. Wilson, Nicholas
D. Wong and Steven Toms

This shortform series presents key peer-reviewed research originally published in the *Journal of Industrial History*, selected by expert series editors and contextualised by new analysis from each author on how the specific field addressed has evolved.

Of interest to business historians, economic historians and social scientists interested in the development of key industries, the series makes theoretical and conceptual contributions to the field, as well as providing a plethora of empirical, illustrative and detailed case studies of industrial developments in Britain, the United States and other international settings.

Growth and Decline of American Industry
Case Studies in the Industrial History of the USA
Edited by John F. Wilson, Nicholas D. Wong and Steven Toms

Banking and Finance
Case Studies in the Development of the UK Financial Sector
Edited by John F. Wilson, Nicholas D. Wong and Steven Toms

Management and Industry
Case Studies in UK Industrial History
Edited by John F. Wilson, Nicholas D. Wong and Steven Toms

The Cotton and Textile Industry: Innovation and Maturity
Case Studies in Industrial History
Edited by John F. Wilson, Steven Toms and Nicholas D. Wong

The Cotton and Textile Industry: Managing Decline
Case Studies in Industrial History
Edited by John F. Wilson, Steven Toms and Nicholas D. Wong

For more information about this series, please visit: www.routledge.com/Routledge-Focus-on-Industrial-History/book-series/RFIH

The Cotton and Textile Industry: Innovation and Maturity

Case Studies in Industrial History

Edited by John F. Wilson, Steven Toms and Nicholas D. Wong

Routledge
Taylor & Francis Group

LONDON AND NEW YORK

First published 2021
by Routledge
2 Park Square, Milton Park, Abingdon, Oxon OX14 4RN

and by Routledge
52 Vanderbilt Avenue, New York, NY 10017

Routledge is an imprint of the Taylor & Francis Group, an informa business

British Library Cataloguing-in-Publication Data
A catalogue record for this book is available from the British Library

Library of Congress Cataloging-in-Publication Data
A catalog record for this book has been requested

ISBN: 978-0-367-02413-0 (hbk)
ISBN: 978-0-367-68400-6 (pbk)
ISBN: 978-0-429-39974-9 (ebk)

Typeset in Times New Roman
by Apex CoVantage, LLC

Contents

Contributors

Roger Holden has written extensively about the Lancashire cotton textiles industry, and especially its architecture and heritage. Roger is an electronics engineer by training, having worked for Ferranti since leaving university, and conducted all of his research in his spare time. Amongst his many works is *Stott and Sons: Architects of the Lancashire Cotton Mill* (1997) and *Manufacturing the Cloth of the World* (2017).

Stephen Procter is the Alcan Professor of Management at the University of Newcastle, UK. His research explores the impact of organisational culture, technology and workplace organisation on economic performance. He has published numerous articles in management and business history journals.

Steven Toms is Professor of Accounting at the University of Leeds, UK. He has published numerous articles on the history of the Lancashire textile industry, and, with David Higgins, edited the volume, *British Cotton Textiles: Maturity and Decline* (2017). He is the author of *Financing Cotton: British Industrial Growth and Decline, 1780–2000* (2020).

Introduction

John F. Wilson, Steven Toms and
Nicholas D. Wong

Volume 4: Contribution and Key Findings

The fourth volume in this series is the first of two that deal with significant issues in the development of the British cotton and textile industries. Together they cover the period between the middle of the nineteenth century and the end of the twentieth century. The current volume considers the pattern of technological innovation in the mature phase of the industry. It offers some explanation as to why Lancashire entrepreneurs were reluctant to emulate international competitors. As a sequel, volume 5 considers how investment decisions taken in the mature phase impacted survival options and strategies during the long period of decline after the First World War.

The chapters of both volumes collectively constitute a significant contribution to the literature on textile history. Since publication, that literature has advanced in several directions which is worth documenting briefly to set the contributions in this volume in the broader perspective. Unlike other volumes in this series, the current volume, along with volume 5, have a single industry focus, and its chapters are commonly impacted by subsequent research. Instead of individual chapter postscripts therefore, this introduction ends with an overarching postscript on their collective contribution.

In the first chapter, on 'Growth, Profit and Technological Choice', Steven Toms examines how entrepreneurs responded to profit signals in formulating their investment and reinvestment decisions. The choices they faced were between traditional intermittent mule spinning, in conjunction with the Lancashire power loom, and continuous ring spinning, developed from the 1870s, in conjunction with the automatic loom, introduced from the 1890s. The latter innovation created the possibility of vertically integrating production, instead of sticking to the traditionally separate and specialised organisation of the industry. Entrepreneurs typically opted for traditional technology and traditional industry structure. They did so not because they were poor decision-makers or preferred less efficient technology and organisation. Rather, integration based on the new technologies was problematic before the 1920s, and vertical specialisation also remained more profitable up to then. The profits generated from traditional structures provided entrepreneurs with more than enough financial muscle to integrate production in large factories, had they chosen to do so. Instead, they exploited the specialised model for all it was worth, diversifying their fortunes into the equity of multiple mills and new flotations. It was this system of finance that went so badly wrong in the final disastrous boom of 1919–1920 and its aftermath.

Roger Holden adds a new, technological dimension to the rings versus mules debate. Notwithstanding the entrenched positions of economists, he argues that the technological history of the industry post-1850 has been neglected. His chapter, 'Ring and Mule Spinning in the Nineteenth Century', shows that ring spindles suffered from several technical deficiencies, reducing their efficiency and adaptability beyond a certain range of specific types of yarn. On both sides of the Atlantic, the ring was developed primarily as a replacement for the throstle spindle, which was an adaptation of Arkwright's water frame. All these methods allowed continuous spinning, as opposed to intermittent mule spinning. Even so, the ring spindle lacked the technical finesse of the mule, and relied upon unskilled labour, mostly for high-frequency doffing. Data reveals that in the USA, where ring spinning was most quickly and widely adopted, the system was nonetheless complementary rather than a direct competitor to mule spinning before 1900. American innovators had some success in adapting ring-spun yarn for use in conjunction with new automatic looms. Compared to the USA, however, Lancashire had a much more technically developed and diverse product range, so it was not surprising that they retained the mule for outputs to which it was more suited. Of course, the mule was eclipsed gradually by the ring, but this was very much a twentieth-century phenomenon. Ashton Brothers of Hyde was a vertically integrated firm with a reputation as a progressive firm. Even so, as Holden notes, when Allan Ormerod joined its management team in 1932, it was still committed to mule spinning for certain lines. Across the industry, by 1950, the transition was complete, and the mule was used only for a small range of specialised outputs.

There were further reasons why Lancashire entrepreneurs were reluctant to extend ring spinning in the nineteenth century. Procter and Toms show that whereas it saved on raw material costs and offered higher gross margins, it was more labour intensive. Employers, therefore, faced higher wage costs at a time of labour scarcity and, by the 1890s, increasing militancy. Mule spinning, with its well-established wage lists and craft trade unions, offered potentially more stable trading conditions. When the industry returned to generally boom conditions after 1896, the increased returns accrued to capital in the form of higher profits, not labour in the form of higher wages. In these circumstances, it is not surprising that there was an investment boom directed mostly into new and larger mule spinning mills after 1900. Whether these investment decisions were correct or not, the evidence does not support the view that organised labour acted as a brake on innovation in the cotton industry.

Taken together, the articles show that vertical integration before 1914 was a straw man, and that horizontal structure supported both technical innovation and export success. Rather, entrepreneurs responded rationally to product and market conditions and the profit signals that were generated accordingly. The consequences were nonetheless an industry that proved too large for the conditions that prevailed after 1918, and the responses to the challenges of this new era are dealt with in volume 5.

The chapters in the present volume and volume 5 were published towards the end of two decades of international research centred on firm organisation and entrepreneurship in the Lancashire textile industry. Mass and Lazonick (1990) published an interim summary in their 'state of the debates' article. Their overall conclusions placed Lancashire entrepreneurs in the dock, for their alleged failure to integrate and modernise production. Subsequent research, including the chapters in the present volume, challenged this view, as summarised above, stressing technological and financial rationalisations of entrepreneurial behaviour. These interpretations are complemented by coterminous publications that emphasised the role of the region as a source of competitive advantage (Farnie et al., 2000), and of external economies of scale in technological choice (Broadberry and Marrison, 2002; Leunig, 2001).

These contributions represented the last word on Lancashire, and the focus of research shifted internationally. In 2004, Farnie and Jeremy published *The Fibre that Changed the World*, a wide-ranging international perspective on industrial organisation, technology and technology transfer across three continents over four centuries. Their analysis reaffirmed the central role of cotton in industrialisation and economic development, setting the scene for Beckert's *Empire of Cotton* (2014). His polemical account explains how Liverpool merchants, in particular, operated at the centre of a commanding global network, leveraging institutional support and political influence. Lancashire's decline, therefore, came as countries like India did the same, placing cotton at the centre of nationally organised industrialisation strategies from the second quarter of the twentieth century. None of these accounts belittles the importance of Lancashire, although they do shift the focus from its entrepreneurs. In his 2020 monograph, *Financing Cotton*, Toms switches the focus back to the history of Lancashire businesses.

Drawing on the research presented in this volume with a more extensive and integrated dataset and covering the period 1780–2000, he shows how networks of production, marketing and finance first enabled and later restricted Lancashire's sustainability as an industrial district. Only rarely did market conditions provide favourable opportunities for reorganisation along vertical lines, a point which strongly echoes the conclusions of the present volume.

References

Beckert, S. *Empire of Cotton: A Global History*. New York, 2014.

Broadberry, S. and Marrison, A. 'External economies of scale in the Lancashire cotton industry, 1900–1950', *Economic History Review*, 55 (2002), 51–77.

Farnie, D. and Jeremy, D. *The Fibre that Changed the World: The Cotton Industry in International Perspective, 1600–1990s*. Oxford, 2004.

Farnie, D., Nakaoka, T., Jeremy D., Wilson, J. and Abe, T. *Region and Strategy in Britain and Japan*. London, 2000.

Leunig, T. 'New answers to old questions: explaining the slow adoption of ring spinning in Lancashire, 1880–1913', *Journal of Economic History*, 61 (2001), 439–66.

Mass, W. and Lazonick, W. 'The British cotton industry and international competitive advantage: the state of the debates', *Business History*, 32 (1990), 9–65.

Toms, S. *Financing Cotton: British Industrial Growth and Decline, 1780–2000*. Woodbridge, 2020.

1 Growth, Profits and Technological Choice

The Case of the Lancashire Cotton Textile Industry

Steven Toms

I

Industrial history is necessarily concerned with economic growth and decline. Lancashire cotton textiles provides a classic case study of these processes. From being the vanguard sector of the industrial revolution in the eighteenth and early nineteenth centuries, the industry fell into rapid and terminal decline in the twentieth. Determinants of growth and decline, such as industry structure, profitability, capital accumulation and technological choice have been addressed in previous studies, although certain variables have enjoyed more attention than others.[1] The period 1870–1914 has been regarded by some as a time when Lancashire entrepreneurs made the mistakes that condemned the industry to its subsequent downfall. In particular, they have sought to establish links between industrial organisation and economic decline. As a result, debates on the poor performance of Lancashire cotton textiles have been somewhat dominated by the issues of technology and organisation.[2]

A mythology has thereby developed based on the ostensibly old fashioned attitudes of Lancashire entrepreneurs and commonly believed interpretations concerning incorrect investment decisions, poor leadership and inappropriate industry structure. Accordingly, the evidence below is examined considering the arguments that have dominated typical discussions of Lancashire textiles. Mostly these have concerned choice of technique, primarily between ring and mule spinning.[3] The first is that Lancashire entrepreneurs did not replace mule spindles and power looms with ring spindles and automatic looms to the extent they should.[4] Second, that ring spindles from a relatively early date were more efficient than mules, especially regarding labour cost.[5] Third, and following on from the first two, that industry structure was an important influence on these investment choices.[6] Each of these points will be examined in more detail below. An additional point of reference, hitherto neglected entirely, will be the strategies and profitability of specific companies differentiated by their investment policies.

The business history of Lancashire textiles has thus far not been informed by evidence from financial and accounting sources. Yet such evidence is of relevance to the major areas of discussion and controversy, such as entrepreneurship, technology and structure, and world markets, dealt with by previous histories. Recent work has used this new evidence to re-examine the strategies of Lancashire entrepreneurs and the business networks that facilitated their operation before 1914.[7] The debates concerning technology, structure and world markets are also important in the light of new evidence and the present purpose is to reconsider these issues.

Accounting records, capital market data, and business archives for a sample of cotton companies, form the main body of evidence for this re-examination. (For a list of principal source material, see appendix 1.) Financial performance, growth and financial policy are the three broad aspects of business strategy examined. The first is measured by profitability, taken as return on capital employed (ROCE), defined as profit before interest as a percentage of long term capital invested. Growth is measured by accumulation of equity capital employed and financial policy refers to principal sources of debt and equity finance for investment, together with the extent of divestment by capital repayments and dividends. The sample is segmented by ownership, vertical structure and choice of technology.

The discussion below uses a political economy framework[8] to examine the development of the cotton economy of Lancashire. Within this framework, the use of accounting and financial data facilitates an examination of the shareholder and manager governance relationship, and the impact of profits and wealth changes in one period and growth and investment in the next. Political economic analysis also moderates some of the difficulties of following an accounting based method, for example the presupposition of capital market efficiency.[9] Publications of accounting numbers are treated as historical events and form a body of empirical evidence for judging the behaviour and response of entrepreneurs and investors. Accounting techniques may have been relatively primitive, but the purpose here is to examine what was reported under historical conditions, rather than what would have been reported under modern conditions.

None of the evidence considered to date has included any case studies of the experience of actual companies, nor reference to the profitability of those companies that shifted to the less familiar technology. To what extent, therefore, were Lancashire entrepreneurs genuinely reticent in experimenting with ring spinning and the automatic loom, and if so why? Was any such reticence justified, and if so, did it ultimately cost the industry its world leadership? To address these questions, the actual experiences of Lancashire companies are examined. The analysis is divided into four sections, which link previous explanations with a framework for empirical evidence introduced by this research. First, the special characteristics of Lancashire entrepreneurship are defined. Then the diffusion of alternative technologies is examined and examples of companies are identified that sought to specialise in ring spinning or experiment with automatic looms, in some cases from a relatively early date. The diffusion pattern is then explained by reference to the financial performance and factor cost structures of companies pursuing different capital investment policies. The causes and consequences of Lancashire's specialised industry structure are then reassessed. Finally, conclusions are drawn and the implications for our understanding of the process of industrial growth and decline are examined.

II

During the late nineteenth century important changes occurred in the social nature of Lancashire capitalism. As the industry moved from growth to maturity, wealth became increasingly concentrated. Unlike other industries, this did not result in monopoly, cartelisation, concentration and the emergence of large managerial hierarchies. Although it is true that some large firms were formed, they failed to dominate the industry.[10] What makes Lancashire a fascinating case in the period 1890–1914 is that increasing wealth concentration among *individual* owners accompanied increasing specialisation in industry structure.

The process of capital accumulation underpinned the emergence of family and local commercial elites. Growth of reinvested equity capital was highest where private or family control was exercised, for example at Horrockses, Crewdson,[11] and for the small minority of companies that raised finance beyond local Lancashire capital markets. Conversely, companies dependent on regional stock markets tended to reduce in size through capital repayments and dividend distributions.[12] Dramatic increases in capital in the period 1896–1914, exemplified by the rise of capitalists such as John Bunting (1839–1923) and William Birtwistle (1855–1936), accrued to individuals rather than corporations.[13] Bunting typified the Oldham based entrepreneur, using public company flotations as the basis of multiple directorships (Frank Platt, 1890–1955, subsequently managing director of the Lancashire Cotton Corporation (LCC), was a later example),[14] whereas Birtwistle relied on the closely controlled private company.[15] In all cases, profits were divested from established businesses for reinvestment through personal flotation or acquisition of other concerns.[16] Crucially, these funds were channelled through the estates of proprietary capitalists. Strategy formulation remained the exclusive remit of these individuals. Meanwhile, managers fulfilled a limited stewardship function designed to ensure surplus cash flow was remitted to the owner as soon as possible.[17]

Managers functioned merely at plant level and were subjected to interference, close scrutiny and sometimes dismissal by owner-entrepreneurs such as Birtwistle and Edward Fielden (1857–1942).[18] They were trusted with routine mill management and supervised only a small hierarchy. For quoted companies in the Oldham district, the pattern was similar, except that shareholder mistrust of management reflected the traditions of shareholder activism associated with working and middle class investment in the 1860s and 1870s. A series of slumps in share values undermined this ownership structure. In the period 1892–5 an index of representative companies declined almost continuously for 48 months.[19] In length, this bear market amounted to a local equivalent of the Wall Street Crash. Companies relied on partly paid shares and had to make fresh calls to stay in business.[20] Rather than meet these, working and middle class investors chose to sell, accentuating price falls further. By 1896, when the market finally turned, wealthier investors who had bought cheaply made significant gains.[21] Thus, capital ownership centralised around cliques of richer shareholders able to exclude residual shareholders and to impose tighter control on nominee managers.[22] Many were skilled at speculation and company flotation. Much borrowing capacity remained unused, whilst lines of credit increased with the social standing of individual proprietors,[23] confidence in which increased as share values recovered. By the 1900s 'empires of individually controlled mills', on the lines suggested above, whose proprietors possessed ready access to financial resources, became more clearly established.[24]

To some extent, Lancashire's development was regionally distinct and remained separate from the rest of the British economy. The stock market crash of the 1890s came at a time when London industrials moved ahead.[25] Whilst Lancashire exports suffered under high gold prices, London was helped by rising demand in the domestic market.[26] Typically, money was raised locally from the accumulated profits and divestments from other cotton concerns and rarely from the banks, even for working capital.[27] Although corporate independence from banks occurred in other sectors, the combined effect was an absence of demand and investment opportunities for capital from outside the county, thereby continuing a divide that had emerged from the time of industrialisation.[28] Increasing independence of financial capitalists further underpinned the special characteristics of Lancashire entrepreneurship.

These governance mechanisms to an extent confirm an important case of British 'personal capitalism'.[29] However they are also suggestive of a gap in existing interpretations of Lancashire entrepreneurship. In particular, their encapsulation of separate roles for entrepreneurs and managers raises the crucial question of the extent to which these individuals contributed to the decline of the industry, for example their inability to invest in new technology.[30] Sandberg argued that decision makers responded rationally to profit signals[31] and loyalty to the mule was justified by its apparent superiority on counts above 40s.[32] In response, Lazonick argued that entrepreneurship was too narrowly defined, allowing cotton managers to be adjudged successful by reference to their ability to produce a rational or optimal solution given certain constraints. Had entrepreneurs been defined in the Schumpeterian sense, they would have been judged by their ability to remove constraints, for example by vertically integrating as a precursor to introducing ring spinning.[33] As it was, 'vertical specialisation . . . constrained the adoption of modern capital intensive technologies in the . . . two decades or so prior to World War I'.[34] Those feeling the constraints the most closely were managers and production technologists, especially those working in the 1920s and 1930s, and their views were quoted extensively by Lazonick as evidence of barriers to such capital intensive production imposed by vertical specialisation.[35] But these individuals were excluded from decisions on industry organisation by the governance structure described above. The power to restructure the industry and to invest in new technology rested with entrepreneurs; the individual and financial capitalists whose adeptness lay in mobilising financial resources and mill flotation. Any constraint on adoption of more capital intensive production lay in the ownership of capital rather than industry structure *ex ante*. Despite attempts to shift the focus to industrial organisation, entrepreneurial attitudes towards technology remain a highly relevant theme and are explored further through case studies of individual companies in the next section.

III

The first known Lancashire factory dedicated to ring spinning was the New Ladyhouse Cotton Spinning Co. Ltd, registered on 26 April 1877.[36] There followed, in the early 1880s, a group of three companies formed around the original New Ladyhouse Company that became known as the 'Milnrow Ring Spinners'.[37] These small, but highly significant firms, operated in a geographically concentrated cluster, and like the examples referred to earlier, were promoted and owned by the same dominant shareholder group.[38] Figure 1.1 contrasts their performance with specialised mule companies spinning similar counts in nearby Oldham. The pioneering Milnrow ring spinners outperformed mule spinners in nearby Oldham in all periods, and also fine spinning companies such as Barlow and Jones Ltd and later those under the control of the Fine Cotton Spinners and Doublers Association (FCSDA).[39] Furthermore, the variance of stock market returns suggested that the ring spinners were less risky.[40] Given the clear and acknowledged[41] premium to ring spinning, it is surprising that the Milnrow companies were

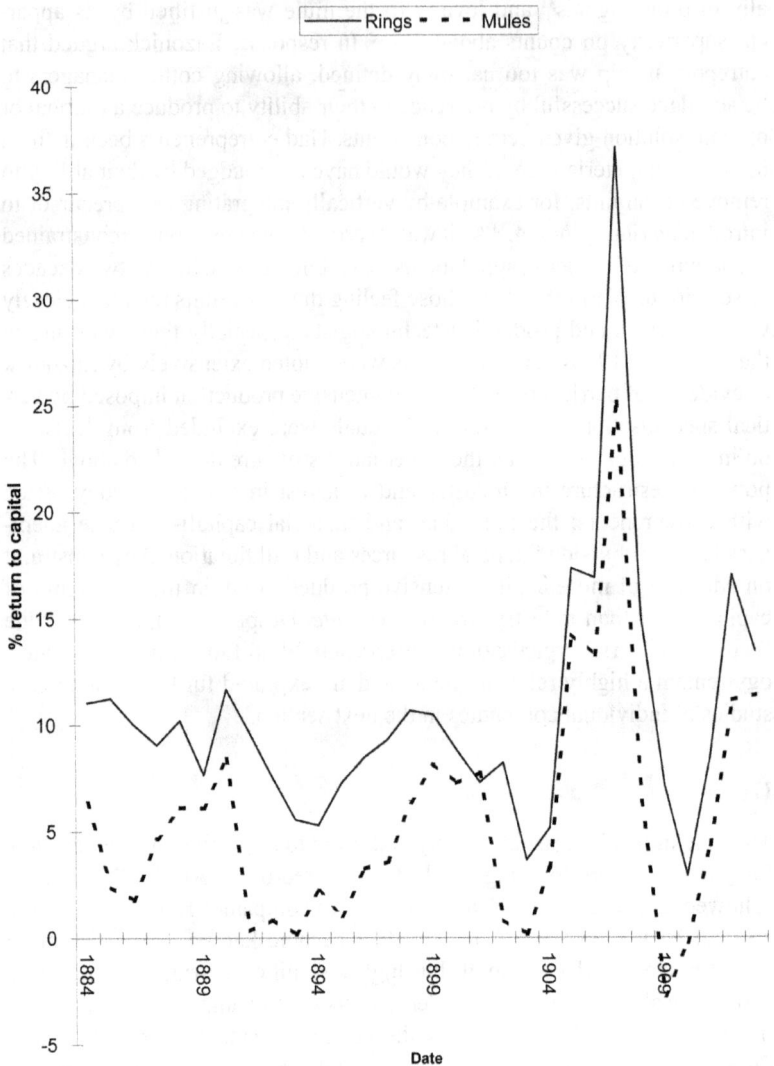

Figure 1.1 Ring and mule spinners' comparative performance.

Sources: Returns calculated for each company listed in appendix 1 and averaged by sub group.

not expanded further in spindleage or capacity and that these early concerns were not more widely emulated in later decades before 1914.

Partly the explanation lies in the inadequacy of the local capital market as a signaling and capital allocation device. Of particular importance was the obsession in Oldham and nearby towns with dividends.[42] According to modern finance theory, where a capital market is efficient, the investor should be indifferent to the proportion of total return received in dividends or capital gains.[43] To an extent, therefore, the dividend obsession must have reflected a degree of market inefficiency. Preferences for immediate cash instead of future capital growth indicated the distrust of managers discussed earlier, and was rational in the sense that it minimised monitoring costs. Also there was a lack of confidence in a relatively thin market,[44] especially in periods such as 1892–5, when difficulties and cost of finding buyers for shares to liquidate investments became a problem for some classes of investor. Specific shareholdings rather than portfolio based investment, and the dominance of 'voice' over 'exit'[45] in most trading conditions fuelled the demand for dividends and prevented the expansion of even the most profitable concerns. Furthermore, the maximisation of dividends, rather than shareholder wealth, cannot have enhanced the allocative efficiency of the market.

Investment decisions were also influenced by entrepreneurial perceptions of risk.[46] In the 1890s, as the coarse trade suffered significant losses in the Indian market, gloom enveloped the industry, with many regarding its prospects with great pessimism.[47] Resulting depression of share values and capital concentration reduced the capital market's operational efficiency and undermined its ability to allocate capital according to rational financial signals in the mill building boom of 1904–7.[48] Meanwhile, whilst the depression lasted, very few new mills of any kind were built in the 1890s, and the diffusion of the ring was undoubtedly slowed by the dampening of expectations. Indeed, little investment of any sort took place, particularly in the depression hit Oldham of the 1890s, and this may be one reason for Oldham's notable commitment to the mule. Mule spindleage in the area declined from 11.4 to 10.9 million spindles between 1891 and 1897.[49] Few other significant ring mill constructions occurred before the early 1900s, notable exceptions being the Palm (1884), specialising in strong rope yarns, the Nile (1898) in Oldham, Burns Ring Spinning Co. Ltd at Heywood (1891) and the Era (1898) in Rochdale.[50]

In many cases capital equipment manufacturers were closely involved with the promotion of new mills. For example, the Milnrow companies and the Era Mill were backed by Howard and Bullough Ltd, whose ring frame was an important addition to its product range, and the Burns company by Samuel Brooks Ltd.[51] In the 1900s the Draper Corporation backed British Northrop Loom Company, in liaison with the Greg, Tootal Broadhurst, and the Hollins family entrepreneurial group fostered similar local experiments in automatic weaving.[52] The backing of such suppliers was common and may have helped underwrite risk, but also reflected interlocked business networks and was thus vital to the diffusion process.[53]

Another reason for limited diffusion was the association of ring spinning with product and geographical specialisation. It was embraced more enthusiastically in some districts, notably Rochdale, than in others, notably Oldham. Traditions of throstle spinning[54] in the former area and the role of capital equipment suppliers and their acquisition of patents, reinforced the local tendency towards specialisation in rings. Despite early patent registration in the USA and in Britain, it was improvements of the Sawyer and Rabbeth spindles from the 1870s and their associated increase in productivity, that encouraged the replacement of throstles with rings in the Rochdale area.[55]

Use of shed style constructions might also have influenced the diffusion of ring spinning into areas such as Rochdale where land prices were lower. The New Ladyhouse mill used such a style and was subsequently emulated by larger ring mills, notably Cromer (1906).[56] In south east Lancashire in the Oldham and Manchester areas, where land was more expensive,[57] it is noteworthy that ring mills built in the 1900s were either smaller, or combined with mule capacity, and availed themselves of the traditional storeyed construction. Capital ownership and the mobilisation of financial resources through local centres such as Oldham, where exercised through the joint stock company, supported larger investment in capital intensive mule companies. These offered substantial economies of scale.[58] Although such economies were present in the large Oldham mule mills of the 1900s, the advantages were less obvious for the smaller ring mills.

It has been argued that the structure of labour relations and the substitution of cheaper inputs was the basis of the survival and indeed success of the mule before 1914. According to this view, Lancashire's success was based on its responses in these areas to the cost cutting strategies of overseas companies, which were armed with the ostensibly advantageous combination of the ring spindle and cheap labour.[59] Again, if the hypothesis is correct, vertically specialised mule mills would be expected to outperform vertically specialised ring mills in Lancashire. Wage cost savings in ring mills would be outweighed by the option of substituting cheaper raw materials in mule mills. Also, there would be additional reasons, associated with packaging and transport costs, to expect the superior performance of the latter.

As the evidence in Table 1.1 and Figure 1.1 suggests, however, although labour cost was higher in ring mills, neither this nor constraints associated with transport and packaging damaged their profitability.[60] In contrast to the mills of Oldham, the ring mills of Rochdale did not provide the allegedly technologically conservative Lancashire entrepreneur with capital-intensive-based competitive advantage.[61] Due mainly to high labour intensity in intermediate processes, in the 1890s labour cost and labour intensity was higher in Rochdale ring mills than their mule equivalents

Table 1.1 Labour cost and intensity in mule and ring mills, 1890–92

	(1) Wages analysis, 1889–90				
	Spind.	*Hands*	*Wages (£)*	*Wages/hand (£)*	*Wages/spind. (£)*
Ring mills					
Haugh	27,200	260	8,692	33.43	0.3196
New Hey	38,000	370	11,802	31.90	0.3106
New Lady-house	15,728	200	5,477	27.38	0.3482
Average				30.90	0.3261
Mule mills					
Hathershaw	77,424	376	9,644	25.65	0.1245
Stanley	48,480	236	7,172	30.39	0.1479
Lees Union	63,000	306	7,048	23.02	0.1119
Dowry	66,670	324	8,244	25.44	0.1237
Average				26.13	0.1270

(2) Comparative cost analysis, early 1890s		
	Ring (%)	*Mule (%)*
Material	70.8	74.7
Labour	13.9	12.9
Depreciation	3.8	3.2
Other	11.5	9.2
	100.0	100.0

(3) Comparative labour intensity in mule and ring mills, 1890	
	spindles/hand
Ring mills	
Haugh	10
New Hey	103
New Ladyhouse	79
Average	96
Mule mills (industry average)	206

Sources: (1) Compiled from, *Oldham Chronicle*, 1st October 1889, *Rochdale Observer*, 28th June 1890 (for mule spinners, in the absence of data on actual hands employed the number was estimated using the industry average of 206 spindles per hand, per G. H. Wood, 'Factory Legislation Considered with Reference to the Wages etc of the Operatives Protected', *Journal of the Royal Statistical Society*, vol. LXVI, 1903, p. 316). Wages data per the quarterly reports of each company, as published in the above newspapers; annual equivalents obtained by multiplying by four. (2) Collation of figures for the same companies as in (1).

in Oldham.[62] Superior profits demonstrated in Figure 1.1 arose from greater efficiency in output per spindle and specialisation through market niches.[63] If labour cost savings did exist, they were confined to the spinning process itself. Ring spinning required more labour in roving and other preparation stages and in after spinning processes, such as doffing and winding.[64] Doffing was an unskilled task, normally assigned to teams (four per machine) of young and inexperienced workers, and their employment no doubt added to the labour intensity of ring spinning.[65] When other entrepreneurs finally began to emulate the Milnrow experiment in the early 1900s, there was little concern with labour saving potentialities.

Ring spinning offered a cheap capital, smaller scale alternative to the mule, but it was to the latter that entrepreneurs turned in the search for economies of scale. After a lag of more than twenty years, the centre of the coarse spinning trade in Oldham to a very limited extent began to copy Rochdale from 1904 onwards. Out of 74 new mills started in the Oldham district between 1900 and 1907,[66] eight were specialist ring spinners. In spindleage terms they were small in relation to mule mills.[67] Nonetheless, ring spinners also became larger, and, unlike the highly specialised large new mule mills, developed higher count product ranges. While the counts spun by the Milnrow group had been 18/36s range in the 1880s and became 6/36s by 1914,[68] the newer companies had average counts of 31s, including some, such as Cromer spinning up to 64s Egyptian and Nile, 80s Egyptian, entering the finer product range.[69] As mule mills exploited economies of scale, for ring spinners product specialisation and market niches were more important, although the ostensible constraint of sub-40s coarse specialisation for ring spindles was far less applicable in the 1900s than it had been in the 1880s.

IV

The previous sections have examined the special characteristics of Lancashire entrepreneurship and some of the reasons why entrepreneurs chose, to a limited degree only, to invest in ring spinning technology. Considering this evidence, it is now useful to reexamine the issue of industry structure and vertical integration, in particular, the hypothesis that the increasing vertical specialisation of the industry became a constraint on the development of high throughput, integrated manufacture.[70] According to this argument, in the rest of the industry both branches began to resist the introduction of new technology because of their structure. Vertical specialisation prevented co-ordinated decision making between spinning and weaving mills necessary for the replacement of power looms with automatic looms because the spinning companies could only supply yarn suitable for the former.[71] Thus, in Britain, only in the production of warp yarns were specialist ring spinners able to compete, since whether rings or mules were used for warp, the yarn still had to be rewound from bobbins onto beams before weaving.[72] If entrepreneurs were concerned to remove the constraints on weft yarn, they could have either installed rings in existing integrated concerns that could also take advantage of developments in automatic weaving, or built brand new integrated factories.

When investment did occur, there were many reasons why entrepreneurs preferred to float specialised rather than integrated concerns. First, as the trends in Figure 1.2 illustrate, to specialise was more profitable during periods of boom. Specialised companies generally performed much better than those companies that perhaps attempted to achieve internal throughput economies through the adoption of vertically integrated structures. One company that almost uniquely followed the strategy of simultaneous investment in ring spinning and automatic looms was Ashton Brothers (another less prominent case was Fielden Bros. Ltd).[73] Whilst the performance of Ashton's was average, specialised ring spinners enjoyed superior profitability. It may have been, however, that in times of depression, integration was a preferred strategy. Thus from Figure 1.2, vertically integrated companies did relatively better in the 1890s than in the 1900s. It was also true that vertical integration was rewarded relative to specialisation in periods of market contraction and penalised in periods of boom for all phases of the trade cycle to 1960.[74] Given such variability and uncertainty, and the absence of permanent periods of advantage to vertically integrated companies, it is not surprising that the integration driven, throughput technology based methods of Ashton's were not emulated, even during the most serious slumps. During the 1930–2 depression, management problems in the early days of the LCC were added to by the sheer scale of a business operating in an industry characterised by relatively small order size and the pedagogic planning problems endemic in centrally allocating these orders to the large number of operating factories.[75] A boardroom battle led to the abandonment of centralised management control in 1932, and its replacement with a profit centre structure. Platt's emergence as managing director ensured that the company remained a relatively decentralised federation of vertically specialised units.[76] As Figure 1.3 illustrates, subsequent under-performance *vis-à-vis* Ashton Brothers was temporary, and reversed by growth phases in the trade cycle, notwithstanding further advances in technology.[77] Accordingly, the argument that entrepreneurs employing capital intensive, throughput technology had more to gain when using ring spinning in integrated production appears illusory.

Secondly, and a reason why the observed profit differentials are not surprising, is that the technical advantages of integrating ring spinning and loom automation were not fully established until the 1920s. In particular,

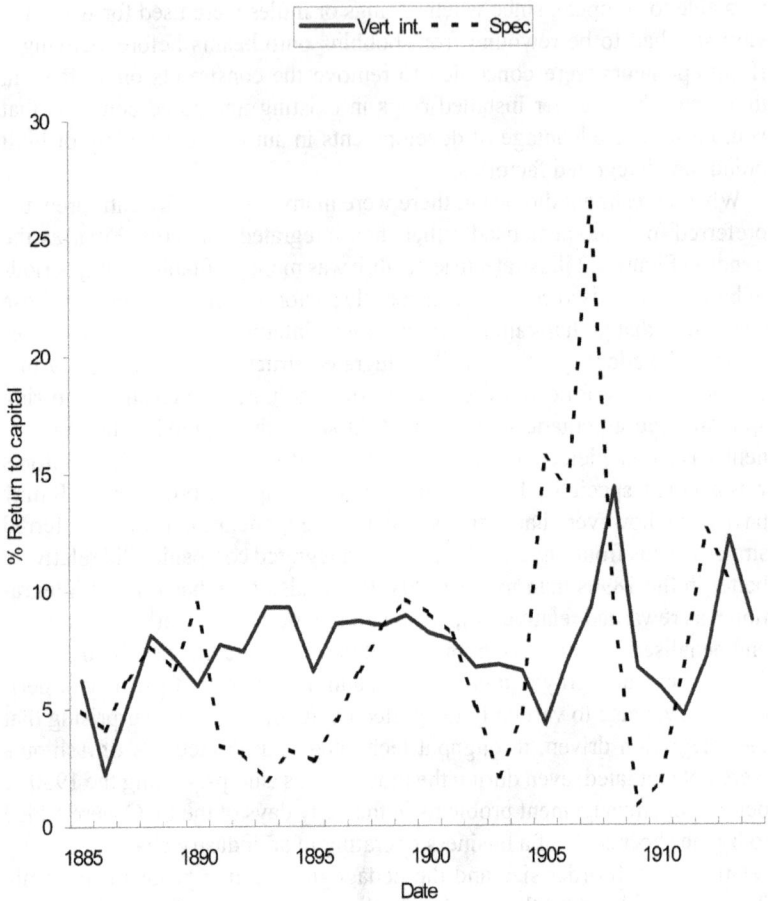

Figure 1.2 Vertically integrated and specialised firms' comparative performance.
Sources: As Figure 1.1

the automation of intermediate processes such as high drafting and high speed winding were important prerequisites of such efficiency gains.[78] Despite the alleged compatibility of ring spinning and automatic weaving prior to 1914,[79] the possibilities for their efficient integrated use were only established by the 1930s. In contrast to gradual developments in continuous spinning, the automatic loom was a steep improvement, and a potentially far more efficient machine than its predecessor. Although vertically integrated companies adopted ring spindles, their financial performance was not

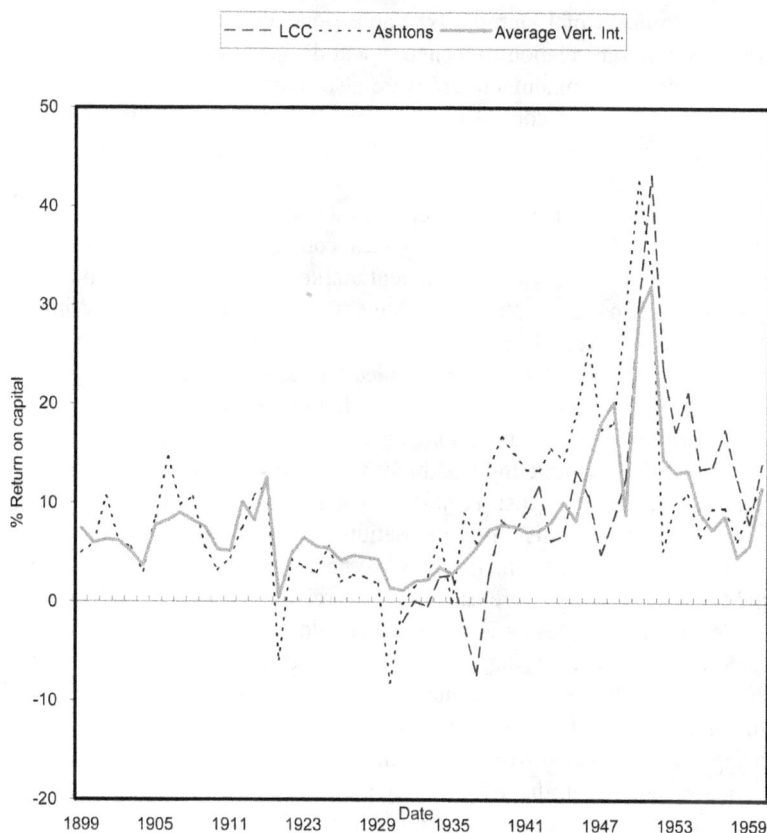

Figure 1.3 Production and organisation strategies - relative profitability

Sources: Adapted from Higgins and Toms, 'Firm Structure', pp. 229–31.

enhanced *vis-à-vis* their specialised competitors (Figure 1.2). Labour intensity at preparation, doffing, and winding stages meant fully automated through-put production was not possible before 1914.[80] Because of labour inten-sity in preparation and doffing, unlike the potential of the new loom, major improvements in ring spinning productivity were not available until after 1914.[81] Experiments with automatic weaving did not therefore necessarily lead to superior profits, despite the greater efficiency of the machines.[82]

Vertical integration was also resisted because entrepreneurs could enjoy its benefits through informal networks without the cost of creating complex organisation structures.[83] An example was the contacts built by most firms with the Liverpool and Manchester markets; particularly the use made by Oldham spinners of Liverpool warehouse operators as cotton stockholders.[84] As noted in relation to technological diffusion earlier, linkages with capital equipment manufacturers were also important. It might be added that because of their control by different entrepreneurial networks, these encouraged either ring or automatic loom installation but not both.

Although factor costs and productivity were important and their emphasis in recent debates is well justified, they do not fully explain performance differentials. Management of integrated companies such as Horrockses and Tootals tended to find that efficient marketing and efficient production worked in opposite directions. Investment in wide product ranges limited the benefits of internal economies of scale in these companies, but especially in the case of Horrockses, provided the basis of sustained competitive advantage via superior profit margins.[85] Internal economies of scale were absent prior to 1914,[86] but also in subsequent periods. To the cotton economy as a whole, marketing was more important than manufacturing efficiency and production costs remained insignificant relative to total cost.[87]

All the above reasons for specialisation were underpinned by the experience of the trade cycle. The British government's commitment to free trade and the gold standard were capable of exercising a dominant influence on the destiny of the industry. For example, the loss and recovery of the Indian market, reflecting lobbying, British electoral arithmetic, and the relationship between the British and Indian governments,[88] had a decisive impact on the development of the coarse spinning American section. First, market changes impoverished working and middle class investors and centralised capital ownership in the 1890s. They then led to the investment boom in specialised concerns during the 1900s backed by the new class of individualistic freelance promotional and speculative capitalists referred to above. (In a parallel process, the 1920s witnessed the impoverishment of the promotional entrepreneurial class and its replacement by the creditor banks.) To all sections of the industry, the world market was vital to profitability and variation in profitability,[89] and entrepreneurs were understandably reluctant to commit themselves to the high fixed costs of big firm organisation.[90] Risk associated with large variations in demand also reduced the value of internal economies of scale.

Finally, the vast returns generated in the days of 'easy money'[91] had an important iterative influence on investor behaviour and reinforced the tendency towards specialisation. This was particularly true of the over-investment in coarse mule spinning capacity during the boom of 1905–7.[92] Perhaps to an extent such entrepreneurial behaviour is to be expected for industries whose output is cyclical around an upward secular trend, as cotton was in the 1900s. Confident expectation of a new and greater boom would no doubt have alleviated the worries of entrepreneurs whose new mills came on stream in 1908 just after the close of the greatest boom hitherto experienced by the industry.

Despite justified optimism, there was a damaging legacy of overcapacity and high cost base that contributed to most subsequent problems of uncompetitiveness. In this sense, the cause of Lancashire's decline was the pattern of capital accumulation during the period of growth. Furthermore, capital ownership became a constraint preventing future investment. There were five reasons for this, all of which would have been relevant in a counterfactual world of widespread vertical integration. First, many of the entrepreneurs who had made money before 1914 had divested through their personal estates by the early 1920s or lost their capital in the slump.[93] Second, after 1920 average profit rates were low, risk perceptions high, and entrepreneurs therefore reluctant to reinvest. Thirdly, such reinvestment had always occurred through new flotation (and re-flotation in the case of the 1919–20 boom) rather than modernisation of existing capacity, and new flotation was not possible due to overcapacity. Fourthly, the overcapacity problem and loss of market share were iterative and compounded difficulties further. Lastly, because of overcapacity reinvestment had to be preceded by scrapping. This raised exit barriers and the opportunity cost of new investment. Thus in some periods after 1920, entrepreneurs used price fixing schemes to support marginal factories creating further market share losses.[94] Meanwhile, serious reorganisation and re-equipment was only countenanced on the basis of external intervention from the Bank of England or the government. The legacy of overcapacity prevented the success of these schemes. In the case of Bank intervention in the 1930s, reorganisation was not helped by the traditional independence of Lancashire from the financial institutions.[95] In the case of government intervention in the 1950s, as suggested by one commentator in 1959, the result was an apparently illogical industrial policy: 'The idea of a subsidy to reduce capacity in order to be eligible for a subsidy to increase it, has a faint flavour of paradox to say the least.'[96] Although the original investments had been made for the best possible reasons, Lancashire unfortunately was not living in the best of possible worlds.

V

There are some obvious limitations to the study presented here, for example, the absence of comparatives with other economies and with other periods.[97] However, the current study has hopefully succeeded in deepening the debate and through introducing new evidence might promote a wider triangulation of views beyond simple economic categories of efficiency. Accordingly, some useful conclusions can be drawn at this stage.

In the above discussion it has been shown that ownership and hence entrepreneurship were important influences on the profitability of and investment in the Lancashire textile industry. In turn, this had an impact on the limited diffusion of ring spinning, although as argued in the final section technological choice was not constrained by industry structure. From the perspective of the entrepreneurial failure hypothesis, it was the character of capital accumulation, rather than the failure of a class of individuals that was important.

Ownership decisively affected growth and industry structure and Lancashire entrepreneurship had several interesting features. Perhaps the most significant was the creation of business empires through personal shareholdings and the ability of entrepreneurs to manage personally relatively large numbers of similar firms. Conversely, they were reluctant to establish professional management hierarchies, which, although increasingly common elsewhere, were compromised in Lancashire by preference for individual, and not corporate, accumulation. The lack of institutional capital accumulation in the industry was, at least in part, a function of the separate development of Lancashire, as an export led manufacturing sector, from the institutional and investment priorities of the British economy as a whole. Ownership of capital thereby became crucial to the development of the industry, with profitability an important determinant of its deployment.

In Schumpeterian terms, the issue was not simply the entrepreneurial removal of constraints, but the broader process of 'creative destruction'.[98] On a broader level still, this was linked to the problem of over-investment described above. The emergent class of pre-1920 entrepreneurs had the purchase of new factories as their hallmark. Given the accumulated financial resources and flotation skills of individuals, and the expansion strategies of some private companies around 1900, there was nothing to stop entrepreneurs investing simultaneously in spinning and weaving capacity.

Why then did these capital rich entrepreneurs not simply eliminate technical interrelatedness constraints by setting up new integrated mills?[99] The answer might be that the industry's markets were growing absolutely before 1914 and that this favoured the entry of more vertically specialised firms.[100] Thus, Lancashire was able during this period to optimise subject to non-problematic constraints of industrial organisation and remain competitive.[101] However, the difficulty with this argument is that Lancashire did not enjoy a smooth growth trajectory before 1914. As discussed earlier, there was a severe depression in the 1890s, characterised by an overvalued currency, loss of market share and serious financial losses for businesses and individuals. Surely if a genuine constraint was imposed by specialisation, it was just as problematic in this period as in the years after 1920? Industry commentators argued, with some justification, that the conditions of the early 1890s paralleled those of the 1920s and early 1930s.[102] Extending the comparison further, if industry organisation was a problematic constraint in the 1920s and 1930s, does it also follow that it again ceases to be problematic in the periods of renewed growth in the late 1930s and after 1945?

To argue that industry structure and labour relations were simultaneously a constraint and non-problematic[103] is a historical contradiction. Remedial action is definable by the hindsight blessed historian and not by the entrepreneur. If, at the time the entrepreneur is supposed to realise a constraint exists, the historian also defines the constraint as non-problematic, it is difficult to see how the entrepreneur can escape the criticisms that have been applied in the case of Lancashire cotton. In reality, there were no structural constraints, and even had they been problematic, the means to eliminate them were also present before 1914, namely the fortunes and reinvestment priorities of individual entrepreneurs. In this sense, the ownership and circulation of capital, not industrial organisation, was the constraint, and as such was only relevant after 1920.

Acknowledgement

I am grateful to Professor S. Tolliday for his scholarly and helpful comments on my thesis 'The Finance and Growth of the Lancashire Textile Industry, 1870–1914' (University of Nottingham, 1996), upon which much of this article is based. I would also like to thank two anonymous referees for their helpful comments on an earlier version of this paper.

Appendix: data and sources

COMPANY	SOURCE
Specialisd Companies	
(1) Mule Spinners	
Crawford	'Commercial Reports', *Oldham Chronicle* (Saturday issues, published summaries of quarterly reports detailing profits, dividends, share and loan capital), April 1884–December 1913.
Dowry	Courtaulds plc Archives, Coventry, LCC/Dow1, Nominal Ledger; June 1885–December 1912; 'Commercial Reports' *Oldham Chronicle*, April 1884–December 1913.
FCSDA	London Guildhall Library (LGL), Commercial Reports, Half Yearly Balance Sheets, 1899–1913.
LCC	Stock Exchange Official Intelligence, 1929–1950; Cambridge University Companies Database, 1950–60.
Moorfield	'Commercial Reports', *Oldham Chronicle*, April 1884 – December 1913; Smith, 'An Oldham Limited Liability Company', pp. 34–53.
Osborne	Lancashire County Record Office (LCRO), DDX/869/3/1, Trade, Capital, and Profit and Loss Accounts, June 1889–June 1914.
Sun Mill	'Commercial Reports', *Oldham Chronicle*, April 1884–December 1913; Tyson, thesis, appendices 1 and 2.
Werneth	Oldham Local Studies Library, Misc. 42/17 and 18, Quarterly Reports to Members, April 1889–October 1912; 'Commercial Reports', *Oldham Chronicle*, April 1884–December 1888.

(2) Ring Spinners

Haugh	'Commercial Reports', *Oldham Chronicle*, April 1884–December 1913; *Rochdale Observer*, 28 June 1890 and Quarterly Reports, April 1892–June 1914 inclusive.
New Hey	'Commercial Reports', *Oldham Chronicle*, September 1886–June 1913; *Rochdale Observer*, 28 June 1890 and April 1892–June 1914.
New Ladyhouse	'Commercial Reports', *Oldham Chronicle*, April 1884–December 1913; *Rochdale Observer*, 28 June and April 1892–June 1914.

Vertically Integrated

Armitage (Sir Elkanah)	LGL, Commercial Reports, Yearly Balance Sheets, 1891–1913.
Ashton Bros	LGL, Commercial Reports, Half Yearly Balance Sheets, 1899–1913.
Barlow & Jones	LGL, Commercial Reports, Half Yearly Balance Sheets, 1900–1913.
Fielden	West Yorkshire Record Office (WYRO) C353/475, December 1891–December 1914; 1884–1889, Law, *Fieldens of Todmorden*, Table XVII, p. 129.
Healey Wood	Rossendale Museum, BB614, Balance Sheets, Quarterly Trading and Profit and Loss Accounts and Balance Sheets, April 1907–December 1914; Dividends Ledger, April 1882–December 1914.
Horrockses	CVR, Detailed Accounts, Half Yearly Balance Sheets and Profit and Loss Accounts, November 1887–October 1905; LCRO, DDHs/53, Balance Sheets, Half Yearly Balance Sheets and Profit and Loss Accounts, October 1905–April 1914.
Rylands	LGL, Commercial Reports, Half Yearly Balance Sheets, 1884–1913; Farnie, 'John Rylands of Manchester', pp. 71–2.
T & R Eccles	LCRO, 868/7/1, September 1897–September 1914.
Tootal	Manchester Central Reference Library, M. 461, Board Minutes, Yearly Balance Sheets and Profit and Loss Accounts, July 1888–July 1914.
Whiteley	LCRO, DDX/868/21/5, September 1898–September 1914.

Note: The above show the primary sources from which profit and capital series were constructed; aggregate data from these companies have been used to construct financial indices which are used throughout the text. CVR is an unlisted archive, previously held by Coats Viyella, recently deposited at Lancashire County Record Office (LCRO).

Notes

1 For an analytical survey of these contributions, see A. J. Marrison, 'Indian Summer', in M. B. Rose (ed.), *The Lancashire Cotton Industry: A History Since 1700* (Preston, 1996).

2 For a comprehensive summary of these debates, see W. Mass and W. Lazonick, 'The British Cotton Industry and International Competitive Advantage: The State of the Debates', *Business History*, XXXII (1990), pp. 9–65.

3 The essential difference was that ring spinning was a continuous process, whereas mule spinning was intermittent, with twist inserted only on the outward movement of a wheeled carriage. For a more detailed explanation see L. Sandberg, *Lancashire in Decline* (Columbus Ohio, 1974), pp. 18–20. Although ring spinning eventually supplanted mule spinning, and the automatic loom the traditional power loom, during this period the two technologies coexisted in direct competition.

4 D. H. Aldcroft, 'The Entrepreneur and the British Economy', *Economic History Review*, 2nd Ser. vol. 17 (1964), pp. 113–34.

5 Sandberg, *Lancashire in Decline*, pp. 29–30.

6 W. Lazonick, 'Industrial Organization and Technological Change: The Decline of the British Cotton Industry', *Business History Review*, vol. LVII (1983), pp. 195–236.

7 J. S. Toms, 'Windows of Opportunity in the Textile Industry: The Business Strategies of Lancashire Entrepreneurs 1880–1914', *Business History*, vol. 40 (1), pp. 1–25; J. S. Toms, 'The Supply of and Demand for Accounting Information in an Unregulated Market: Examples from the Lancashire Cotton Mills', *Accounting Organizations and Society*, vol. 23 (2), pp. 217–38.

8 Political economy is the interplay of power, the goals of power wielders and the productive exchange system. M. Zald, 'Political Economy: A Framework for Comparative Analysis', in M. Zald (ed.), *Power in Organisations* (Nashville, 1970), is concerned with the origins and distribution of power in society. B. Jackson, *The Political Economy of Bureaucracy* (Oxford, 1982). For current purposes, although changes in power and influence are held to be functions of changes in wealth, the term political economy is used in a pluralist non-Marxist sense, ie individual interests are not systematically reconstructed as class interests.

9 In an efficient market, prices quickly reflect all available information. Although this may be a more accurate assumption in modern computer-based markets, in historical settings it is less likely to be the case. For example, an efficient market assumption might fail to consider social processes, such as habit and emulation (H. White, 'Where do markets come from?', *American Journal of Sociology*, 1981, p. 518), and historical antecedents, W. Mitchell, *Business Cycles* (California, 1913, p. 86). Market institutions possess social and historical specificity; market processes may require context especially where characterised by disequilibrium. L. Putterman, *The Economic Nature of the Firm* (Cambridge, 1986, p. 16).

10 H. Macrosty, *The Trust Movement in British Industry* (London, 1907).

11 J. S. Toms, 'The Profitability of the First Lancashire Merger: the Case of Horrocks Crewdson, 1887–1905', *Textile History*, 24 (2) (1993), pp. 129–46.

12 J. S. Toms, 'The Finance and Growth of the Lancashire Cotton Textile Industry, 1870–1914', Unpublished Ph.D Thesis, University of Nottingham (1996), chs 7,

8 & 9; Toms, 'Windows of Opportunity', table 1, p. 4; J. S. Toms, 'The Finance and Growth of the Lancashire Cotton Textile Industry, 1870–1914', *Business and Economic History*, vol. 26 (2), pp. 323–9. J. S. Toms, 'Financial Constraints on Economic Growth: Profits, Capital Accumulation, and the Development of the Lancashire Cotton Spinning Industry, 1885–1914', *Accounting Business and Financial History*, vol. 4 (3) (1994), pp. 364–83.

13 Toms, 'Supply and Demand', pp. 226–31; Toms, thesis, chs 8 & 9.

14 D. A. Farnie, 'John Bunting', in D. Jeremy (ed.), *Dictionary of Business Biography* (London, 1984–86). J. Bamberg, 'Sir Frank Platt' (*ibid*). Other examples included T. E. Gartside (Jeremy, *ibid*) and J. B. Tattersall (McIvor, *ibid*), Thomas Henthorn, Harry Dixon, William Hopwood, Ralph Morton, John S. Hammersley, and Sam Firth Mellor (D. Gurr, and J. Hunt, *The Cotton Mills of Oldham*, Oldham, 1989, pp. 9–10).

15 T & R Eccles and Company Ltd, LCRO, 868/20/1, Directors' Minutes and DDX/868/7/1, Profit and loss accounts and balance sheets; Geo. Whiteley and Co. Ltd, DDX/868/21/5, Balance sheets, 1898–1914 and DDX/868/21/1, Directors' Minute Book.

16 Toms, 'Financial Constraints', pp. 364–83; for other examples in the Manchester area, see H. Berghoff, 'Regional Variations in Provincial Business Biography: The Case of Birmingham, Bristol and Manchester, 1870–1914', *Business History*, vol. 37 (1995), p. 76.

17 In addition to dividends, high withdrawals occurred through directors' emoluments in private companies such as Fielden (WYRO, C353/475, Detailed Accounts, 1890–1914), and sales commission, for example in the Birtwistle companies (LCRO, 868/7/1, Profit and Loss Accounts and Balance Sheets, 1897–1931).

18 Fielden Brothers Ltd provides a useful case study of sometimes technically proficient managers being dismissed by proprietors relying on knowledge of markets, position and profit margins to manage the business; J. S. Toms, 'Integration, Innovation, and the Progress of a Pennine Cotton Enterprise: Fielden Brothers Ltd. 1889–1914', *Textile History*, vol. 27 (1996), pp. 77–100; B. Law, *Fieldens of Todmorden: A Nineteenth Century Business Dynasty* (Littleborough: George Kelsall, 1995).

19 A simple average index of 20 Oldham companies, selected from the *Oldham Chronicle* share listing and with a value of 100 at June 1890 had fallen to 50.2, its pre-war low, by March 1896. An index for industrial companies quoted on the London stock exchange, K. C. Smith and G. F. Horne, 'An Index Number of Securities, 1867–1914', *London and Cambridge Economic Service*, Special Memorandum, No. 37 (1934), columns 1–10, pp. 14–15, showed corresponding figures of 100 and 128.3.

20 W. Thomas, *The Provincial Stock Exchanges* (London, 1973), p. 147.

21 In a couple of years, 1896 and 1897, investor returns were two and three hundred percent. For example, the Albert saw a rise in its shares from 1s and 6d to 15s 6d in just over a year, *Oldham Chronicle*, 28 September 1895; 26 December 1896; Toms, thesis, p. 110.

22 For example at Sun Mill; R. E. Tyson, 'Sun Mill: A Study in Democratic Investment', unpublished M.A. Thesis, University of Manchester (1962), pp. 294–5; Toms, 'Supply and Demand', p. 229.

23 F. Jones, 'The Cotton Spinning Industry in the Oldham District from 1896–1914' Unpublished M.A. thesis, University of Manchester (1959); for example the Times No. 2 Mill floated by Bunting had using £250,000 loan capital on only £8,000 equity, pp. 87–8.

26   *Steven Toms*

Toms, thesis, ch. 9; in the flotation boom of 1905–7, the paid up capital of new companies was issued to relatively few shareholders; Thomas, *The Provincial Stock Exchanges*, p. 155. Those shareholders in turn made significant investments in several mills, and in many cases bought themselves into board positions; Toms, 'Supply and Demand', p. 230; Tyson, 'Sun Mill', p. 299.
25 Toms, thesis, p. 406.
26 Toms, thesis, ch. 11.
27 Toms, 'Windows of Opportunity', table 3.
28 J.B. Jefferys, 'Trends in Business Organisation in Great Britain since 1856, with Special Reference to the Financial Structure of Companies, the Mechanism of Investment and the Relations between the Shareholder and the Company', Ph.D. thesis (London: London University, June 1938); the evidence from Lancashire informs further a broader discussion of separate development. See for example G. Ingham, *Capitalism Divided? The City and Industry in British Social Development* (London, 1984) and W.D. Rubinstein 'Modern Britain', in *idem* (ed.), *Wealth and the Wealthy in the Modern World* (London, 1980).
29 A. D. Chandler, *Scale and Scope: The Dynamics of Industrial Capitalism* (Cambridge, Mass., 1990), p. 240.
30 Chandler, *Scale and Scope*, p. 333.
31 As Figure 1.1 makes clear, profit signals varied dramatically through time – a point not fully dealt with in Sandberg's analysis.
32 D. McCloskey and L. Sandberg, 'From Damnation to Redemption: judgements on the late Victorian entrepreneur', *Explorations in Economic History*, Winter 1971–72, vol. 9 (1972), p. 100; Sandberg, *Lancashire in Decline*, p. 28. The fineness of yarn was measured by the count(s), the ratio of hanks to the pound.
33 Lazonick, 'Industrial Organization', pp. 232–6.
34 Lazonick, 'Industrial Organization', pp. 204–5.
35 For example, F. Holt, J. Kershaw and B. Robinson, *Journal of the British Association of Managers of Textile Works*, 1929–30, 1912–13, 1918–19 respectively; cited in Lazonick, 'Industrial Organization', pp. 205 and 207.
36 Rochdale Local Studies Library (RLSL), New Ladyhouse Cotton Spinning Co. Ltd, Memorandum and Articles of Association; 'Milnrow Ring Spinning Companies', *Rochdale Observer*, 28 June 1890, p. 4.
37 The mills were in the township of Milnrow south east of Rochdale and north west of Oldham. Ring spinning developed from the earlier throstle which in turn dated back to the continuous spinning of Arkwright's water frame; W. Murphy, *The Textile Industries: A Practical Guide to Fibres, Yarns and Fabrics* (London, 1910), vol. 3, p. 68, M. Copeland, 'Technical Development in Cotton Manufacturing Since 1860', *Quarterly Journal of Economics*, vol. 24 (1909), pp. 122.
38 'Milnrow Ring Spinning Companies', *Rochdale Observer*, 28 June 1890, p. 4.
39 Toms, 'Windows of Opportunity', table 2.
40 For the period 1884–1913, the average stock market return for ring spinners was 10.9% with a standard deviation of 11.1%, compared to mule spinners with 13.82% and 33.08% respectively; Toms, thesis, p. 89.
41 Commenting on the profit per spindle results for 1890, in a table showing the Milnrow group at 1st, 2nd and 4th positions, an *Oldham Chronicle* correspondent wrote: 'The ring spindle concerns lead the way as usual . . .', 3 January 1891.
42 The dividend propensities of limited companies created a local perception that the companies existed primarily for the purpose of paying dividends and nothing more, earning Oldham the nickname of 'Diviborough'. D. Farnie, *The English Cotton Industry and the World Market* (Oxford: Clarendon Press 1979), p. 263.

43 M. H. Miller and F. Modigliani, 'Dividend Policy, Growth and the Valuation of Shares', *Journal of Business*, vol. 34 (1961), pp. 411–33.

44 Thomas, *The Provincial Stock Exchanges*, p. 155.

45 Shareholders preferred the 'voice' mechanism of scrutinising management at quarterly meetings rather than the 'exit' option of selling their shares, as defined in A. Hirschman, *Exit, Voice and Loyalty* (Boston, 1970). See also Toms, 'Supply and Demand', pp. 223–4.

46 The Rochdale experiments were described as a 'leap in the dark, involving great risk', *Rochdale Observer*, 28 June 1890.

47 'Is the Cotton Trade Leaving the Country?', *Textile Mercury*, 21 January 1893, p. 43.

48 In the early 1900s, stock market returns for mule spinners outpaced ring spinners. Toms, thesis, pp. 87–8.

49 D. A. Farnie, 'The emergence of Victorian Oldham as the Centre of the Cotton Spinning Industry', *Saddleworth Historical Society Bulletin*, vol. 12 (1982), p. 42.

50 For a list of newly floated mills, see Jones, thesis, pp. 221–3; for Palm Mill see the company's advertisement in the annual editions of J. Worrall, *The Cotton Spinners and Manufacturers Directory for Lancashire* (Oldham); for Era Mill see Era Ring Mill Company Ltd, *History of the Era Ring Mill* (Rochdale, undated), p. 1.

51 *Rochdale Observer*, 4 January 1890. I am grateful to D. A. Farnie for information on the Burns Mill.

52 M. B. Rose, *The Gregs of Quarry Bank Mill* (Cambridge, 1986); Toms, 'The First Lancashire Merger', pp. 129–46; Toms, thesis, ch. 6.

53 Toms, 'Windows of Opportunity'.

54 *Textile Recorder*, 13 May 1897, attributed the spread of ring spinning in Rochdale to the previous tradition of throstle spinning; see also *Cotton Factory Times*, 26 March 1897.

55 These advances stimulated the adoption of ring spinning internationally; G. Saxonhouse and G. Wright, 'Rings and Mules around the World', *Research in Economic History*, Supplement 3 (1984), p. 289. In England, prior to these developments, capital equipment manufacturers concentrated on the further 'perfection' of the flyer throstle (*Rochdale Observer*, 4 January 1890).

56 *Rochdale Observer*, 28 June 1890, p. 4; D. A. Farnie, 'The Cotton Towns of Greater Manchester', in M. Williams, with D. A. Farnie, *Cotton Mills in Greater Manchester*, Royal Commission on Historical Monuments (1992), p. 44; Farnie, *English Cotton*, p. 230.

57 T. Leunig, 'The Myth of the Corporate Economy' (unpublished PhD thesis, University of Oxford, 1996), p. 144.

58 S. Kenney, 'Sub regional specialization in the Lancashire cotton industry, 1884–1914: A study in organizational and locational change', *Journal of Historical Geography*, vol. 8 (1982), p. 59.

59 W. Lazonick, 'Production Relations, Labor Productivity, and Choice of Technique', *Journal of Economic History*, vol. XLI (1981), pp. 512–13, W. Lazonick and W. Mass, 'The Performance of the British Cotton Industry, 1870–1913', *Research in Economic History*, vol. IX (1984), p. 5.

60 Leunig, thesis; transport costs were relatively insignificant and were unlikely to have increased costs of vertically specialised ring spinners.

61 Sandberg, *Lancashire in Decline*, p. 30.

62 Toms, thesis, ch. 5.

63 In 1890, there were 400,000 ring spindles installed in the Rochdale district, producing a weekly output 17,200,000 hanks (*Rochdale Observer*, 4 January 1890), or the equivalent of 43 per spindle. The comparable output of a mule spindle in 1893 was 31 hanks (T. Thornley, *Modern Cotton Economics*, London, 1923, p. 302). With the emergence of the cotton industry Rochdale began to specialise in flannels and flannelettes, the latter being introduced in 1883. The district also specialised in supplying strong yarns, eg for tyres to the motor industry (Farnie, 'Cotton Towns', p. 44).

64 J. Winterbottom, *Cotton Spinning Calculations and Yarn Costs* (London, 1921), p. 261. J. Jewkes and E. M. Gray, *Wages and Labour in the Lancashire Cotton Spinning Industry* (Manchester, 1935), p. 129.

65 C. Kenney, *Cotton Everywhere: Recollections of Northern Women Mill Workers* (Bolton, 1994), pp. 130–1. The New Ladyhouse had a spindles to operative ratio of 79; a ring spinning mill in France in 1882 producing 30s twist had a spindle per operative ratio of 75. F. Merrtens, 'The Hours and Cost of Labour in the Cotton Industry at Home and Abroad', *Transactions of the Manchester Statistical Society* (1894), p. 160; the comparable figure for mule spinning was 205, derived from G. Wood, 'Factory Legislation Considered with Reference to the Wages of the Operatives Protected', *Journal of the Royal Statistical Society*, LXV (1902), p. 316.

66 Jones, thesis, p. 223.

67 Belgrave 2 had only 43,200 spindles, although Iris (62,568), Moston Ring (59,796) and Royton Ring (64,176) were more typical. By contrast, the median mule specialist in the Oldham district was by this time of the order of 100–130 thousand spindles. The largest, Times No. 2, at 174,000 spindles, revealed the limits of economies of scale in the mule section, see Jones, thesis, p. 88, 221–3. This size difference persisted into the 1930s. See G. Bennett, 'The Present Position of the Cotton Industry in Great Britain' (unpublished MA thesis, University of Manchester 1933).

68 Worrall, *Cotton Directory*, 1891 and 1913. Below 40s are usually taken to be coarse yarns.

69 Jones, thesis, pp. 221–3.

70 W. Lazonick, 'Competition, Specialization and Industrial Decline', *Journal of Economic History*, vol. XLI (1981), pp. 31–8.; W. Lazonick, 'Industrial Organization and Technological Change', pp. 195–236; W. Lazonick, 'The Cotton Industry', in B. Elbaum and W. Lazonick (eds), *The Decline of the British Economy* (Oxford 1986).

71 Lazonick, 'Competition, Specialization and Industrial Decline', pp. 33–4. M. Frankel, 'Obsolescence and Technical Change in a Maturing Economy', *American Economic Review*, June (1955), p. 213.

72 W. Lazonick, 'Stubborn Mules: some comments', *Economic History Review*, 2nd ser., XL (1987), p. 82.

73 Lazonick, 'Industrial Organization', p. 211; Toms, thesis, ch. 6.

74 D. M. Higgins and J. S. Toms, 'Firm Structure and Financial Performance: The Lancashire Textile Industry', *Accounting Business and Financial History*, vol. 7 (1997); pp. 195–232.

75 Bennett, thesis, p. 77.

76 Bamberg, 'Sir Frank Platt', pp. 717–19; *Economist*, 8 October 1932.

77 That the LCC succeeded in making even small profits in the 1930s is surprising; the company had to bear a burden of inefficient capacity that should have been shared across the industry. A. Lucas, *Industrial Reconstruction and the Control of Competition* (London, 1937), p. 156.

78 G. Saxonhouse and G. Wright, 'Stubborn Mules and Vertical Integration: the disappearing constraint', *Economic History Review*, 2nd Ser. vol. XL (1987), p. 92; Toms, thesis, ch. 5.

79 Lazonick, 'Industrial Organization', p. 205.

80 High drafting was a significant technical solution, but not widely available until the 1920s; S. Noguera, *Theory and Practice of High Drafting* (privately published, 1936).

81 Higgins and Toms, 'Firm Structure and Financial Performance', p. 213; in the period 1893–1915, both ring and mule spinning had average productivity improvements of 0.08% per year contrasting with high draft ring spinning installations of the 1930s which resulted in improvements in labour productivity of 42%, 56% and 50%; see also Thornley, *Modern Cotton Economics*, p. 302 and Board of Trade, *An Industrial Survey of the Lancashire Area (Excluding Merseyside)* (London, 1932), p. 135.

82 Toms, 'Fielden Brothers', pp. 91–5; Toms, thesis, pp. 175–92.

83 Toms, 'Windows of Opportunity'; Higgins and Toms, 'Firm Structure and Financial Performance', pp. 216–17.

84 D. A. Farnie, *The Manchester Ship Canal and the Rise of the Port of Manchester, 1894–1975* (Manchester, 1980), pp. 74–5.

85 Toms, 'The First Lancashire Merger', pp. 132–3; Toms, thesis, ch. 6.

86 Lazonick and Mass, 'British Cotton Industry', pp. 16–17.

87 Higgins and Toms, 'Firm Structure and Financial Performance', pp. 219–20; Marrison, 'Indian Summer', p. 264.

88 E. Green, 'Rentiers versus producers? the political economy of the Bimetallic controversy, *c*. 1880–98', *English Historical Review*, CIII, July (1988), p. 588; see also the further discussion in A. C. Howe, 'Bimetallism, *c*. 1880–1898: A Controversy Re-opened', *English Historical Review*, CV, April (1990); Toms, thesis, ch. 11.

89 Toms, thesis, ch. 11.

90 Lucas, *Industrial Reconstruction*, p. 167.

91 B. Bowker, *Lancashire under the Hammer* (London, 1928).

92 Toms, thesis, ch. 10.

93 For example, Platt retired temporarily after the re-flotation boom of 1920; Bamberg, 'Sir Frank Platt', p. 716; in contrast, James Henry Bunting (1874–1929), son of John, lost much of his inherited capital in the depression, D. A. Farnie, 'John Bunting' in Jeremy (ed.), *DBB*, p. 508.

94 H. Clay, *The Problem of Industrial Relations* (London, 1929), p.137.

95 M. Dupree, *Lancashire and Whitehall: The Diary of Sir Raymond Streat*, vol. 1, 1931–39 (Manchester, 1987), p. 34.

96 *The Accountant*, 2 May 1959, p. 539.

97 But see Higgins and Toms, 'Firm Structure and Financial Performance', pp. 195–232.

98 J. A. Schumpeter, *Capitalism, Socialism and Democracy* (London, 1976; first published, 1942), ch. 7.

99 A similar question was asked of Lazonick by Saxonhouse and Wright, 'Stubborn Mules', pp. 87–8.

100 Lazonick, 'Industrial Organization', p. 203.

101 Mass and Lazonick, 'British Cotton Industry', p. 57.

102 Federation of Master Cotton Spinners' Associations, *Measures for the Revival of the Lancashire Cotton Industry*, Manchester, F.M.C.S.A. (1936).

103 Mass and Lazonick, 'British Cotton Industry', p. 57.

2 Ring and Mule Spinning in the Nineteenth Century

A Technological Perspective

Roger Holden

The supremacy of the Lancashire cotton spinning industry in the nine-teenth century and up to 1914 was built on the spinning mule and it was this machine that enabled the industry to process a wide range of cottons sourced from different parts of the world into a wide range of yarns from the very coarsest to those finer than anything spun in the world today and for varied purposes such as weaving, knitting and thread making. But in the twentieth century the industry went into decline and today no cotton is spun in Lancashire. Moreover, where cotton is spun, mainly in Asia, it is not spun on mules but on ring frames, and to a lesser extent on open-end rotors. The current study arose out of a desire to understand the technol-ogy of the Lancashire cotton spinning industry which led to the investiga-tion of the technological issues behind the seemingly slow development of ring spinning. But one cannot do this without encountering the classic 'rings versus mules' debate which has been pursued by economic histo-rians since the 1960s. The fundamental argument was that a major factor in Lancashire's decline in comparison with other countries, particularly the United States of America, was that the industry had not adopted the ring frame to the extent that it should have done. The debate was revital-ised in the 1980s with the publication of papers by William Lazonick and others who argued that the structure of the industry prevented the wider adoption of ring spinning and that the industry had failed because it had not restructured itself for the use of ring spinning in integrated mills.[1] This debate is not dead, since more recently other scholars have dealt with the question, while providing differing view points on the decline of the Lancashire cotton industry. For example, Steven Toms has brought evidence from financial and accounting records to bear on the problem, while Stephen Broadberry and Andrew Marrison have argued in favour of the traditional view that Lancashire's decline was primarily the result of foreign competition based on cheap labour.[2] They, and other writers, also point out that the New England cotton industry, which made extensive use of ring spinning in integrated mills, failed even more catastrophically than Lancashire during the inter-war years.[3]

However, bearing in mind Sheila Mason's point that, in the context of the machine lace industry, lack of technological knowledge can be a hindrance to understanding the history of an industry, a survey of the literature will show that the technological factors bearing on the choice between mule and ring spinning in the Lancashire cotton industry have not been adequately studied.[4] While a considerable amount of work has been published in the last two decades on the industrial archaeology of the textile industry, this has not been accompanied by any new research into the history of textile engineering.[5] The early inventions in cotton spinning have been exhaustively studied and the work by Richard Hills is still the definitive account.[6] The volume on the textile industry in Longman's Industrial Archaeology series again concentrates on early inventions, and says very little about developments after about 1850.[7] Harold Catling wrote a clear technical description of the spinning mule which also considers ring spinning as a rival system, but is historically unreliable.[8] A survey of relevant journals shows that the few papers that have been published are biased towards the early inventions. This is true of both the *Transactions of the Newcomen Society,* which has published no papers on textile engineering since the 1960s, and *Textile*

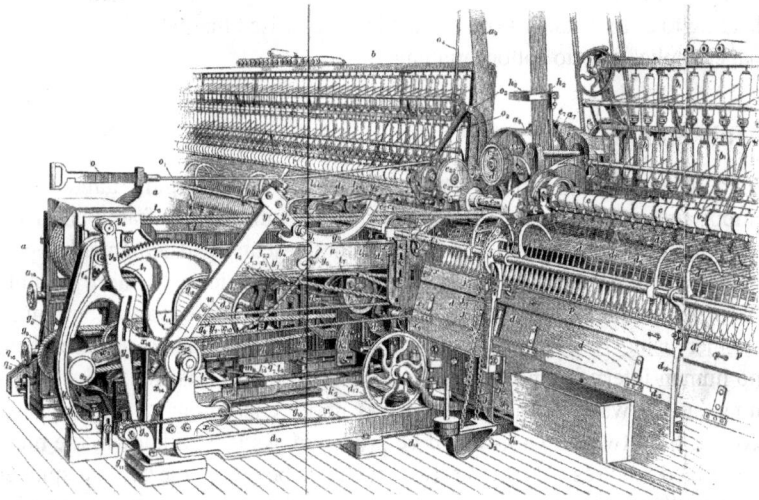

Figure 2.1 Self-acting spinning mule by Asa Lees & Co. Ltd of Oldham.

(*Source:* 'Cotton Mules, Part 1', in *ICS Reference Library, vol. 64* (London: International Correspondence Schools Ltd, 1905), fig. 1.)

History, whose stated scope does in fact cover technological development but has published nothing in this field for over two decades.[9]

Therefore, the present paper seeks to develop an understanding of the development of ring spinning, showing that there were technological reasons for its slow introduction. Methodologically, this will demonstrate that, although the understanding of technology may be easier for engineers than historians, technological history is an important component of industrial history. The major sources for this study have been contemporary publications, patents and records of the textile machine makers in the Platt-Saco-Lowell archive at the Lancashire Record Office. Mule spinning is first considered to show how the original hand mule was a machine of great versatility. The problems in developing a self-acting mule were essentially problems in kinematics and over a period of several decades the self-acting mule was developed to spin the whole range of yarns, but in doing so became a machine of great complexity. The second section deals with the development of the ring frame and its origins as a replacement not for the mule but for the throstle. The third section shows how although, by contrast with the mule, the ring frame is in essence a simple automatic machine, it had a number of serious dynamic problems, particularly that of spindle balancing, which needed to be solved before it could spin more than a restricted range of yarns and seriously challenge the mule. A fourth section shows that the ring frame was readily taken up in Lancashire for spinning types of yarn to which it was particularly suited, followed by a brief outline of the ultimate success of ring spinning in the twentieth century, leading to a final conclusion. It must be emphasised that what is said in this paper applies only to cotton spinning.

Mule Spinning

First, it is important to understand why mule spinning rapidly gained such importance in Lancashire and eclipsed Arkwright's water frame and Hargreaves' spinning jenny. Hargreaves' spinning jenny was a manually operated intermittent spinner using spindle drafting which was more suitable for woollen than cotton yarns. Arkwright's water frame was a continuous spinner using roller drafting which was totally mechanical in operation, no human intervention was required nor indeed was possible. When spinning on the water frame the yarn was under continuous tension so only coarse, hard-twisted yarns could be produced. As is well known, the mule combined features of the other two machines being an intermittent spinner using roller drafting which was manually operated. This gave it four major advantages over the other machines enabling a wider range of high quality yarns to be produced. First, the yarn was not under tension during spinning so very fine yarns could be produced. Second, although the rollers would do most of the drafting, it was possible to also introduce spindle drafting either by moving the carriage faster than yarn was delivered by the rollers or by halting delivery from the rollers before the carriage had finished moving outwards. This is important because roller drafting by itself cannot produce a totally regular yarn and application of spindle draft will even out the irregularities. Thirdly, on a mule the amount of roller drafting, the amount of spindle drafting and the amount of twist can all be independently varied. Fourthly, the mule produced a cop, a yarn package which did not require a bobbin as in the water frame and could be inserted directly into the loom shuttle, allowing yarn to be drawn off without rotating the cop. Thus the mule could spin the whole range of yarns, from coarse to fine, from highly twisted warp yarns to lesser twisted weft yarns and all to a very high quality in terms of evenness of yarn.

Mule spinning was in origin a totally manual process (Figure 2.2). The advantage of this was that the application of human skill enabled a wide range of yarns to be produced, but the disadvantage was that productivity was limited by the power of human muscles. The requirement for skilled operatives increased cost, while the total dependence on human skill would have presented problems in ensuring consistency of the final product. Application of power to the first, spinning, part of the cycle was relatively easy and had been achieved about ten years after invention of the mule. This included mechanisms to stop the drafting rollers when a sufficient length of yarn had been delivered, to halt the carriage at the end of its run and to halt rotation of the spindles when the correct amount of twist had been put in.

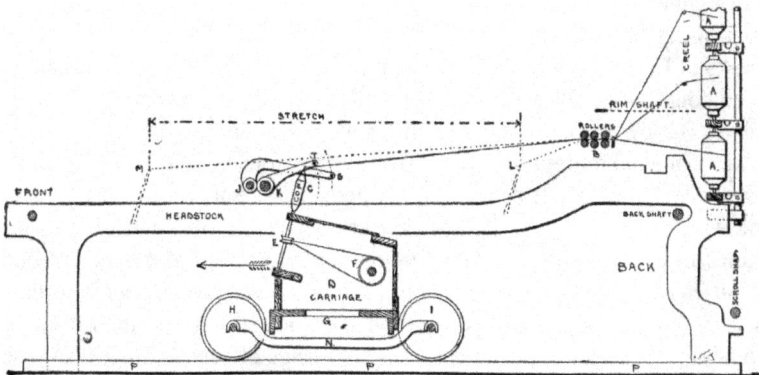

Figure 2.2 The mule spinning system. Yarn is spun on the outward movement of the carriage and wound-on during the inward movement.

(*Source:* William Scott-Taggart, *Cotton Spinning, vol. 3* (London: Macmillan & Co. Ltd, 5th edn, 1938), fig. 10.)

William Kelly of New Lanark may have been the first to achieve this and such mechanisms are included in his patent of 1792 which describes a complete self-acting mule.[10] However, Kelly's mechanisms for automating the second, winding, part of the cycle did not work and this proved far more difficult to automate. The problem was solved in principle by Richard Roberts in his patents of 1825 and 1830.[11] The long time taken to solve this problem was not through want of trying as several patents were taken out in the intervening period.[12] As is well known, the key to Roberts' success was the quadrant mechanism which controlled spindle speeds during the winding part of the cycle. This replicated closely the control that would be carried out by a hand spinner. But another important feature of Roberts' design was that he provided separate drives to the carriage and to the spindles during the spinning and winding parts of the cycle, thus adding to the complexity of the self-acting mule.

But although Roberts had basically solved the problems of building a self-acting mule, it took a long time before all yarns up to the finest could be spun on these machines and, so-called, hand mules continued to be produced. These hand-mules were powered over the spinning part of the cycle, the spinner then taking over to back-off and control winding while 'putting-up' the carriage, although power came to be applied to assist the spinner in this. Fine yarns could not, of course, stand so much strain as coarse yarns while greater accuracy was needed in winding to ensure a tightly wound cop and that no snarls were left at the end of winding. The yarn was under most strain during the backing-off part of the mule cycle. However, textile machinists applied their skills to solving these problems and as the nineteenth century progressed finer and finer yarns could be spun using self-acting mules. This can be illustrated from the mule order books of Dobson & Barlow Ltd.[13] Table 2.1 shows the number of orders in each count range for hand and self-acting mules in the year 1856.[14] Dobson & Barlow were producing mules for the Bolton fine-counts trade and orders for hand mules predominate over orders for self-actors and there is a clear division with self-actors being ordered for counts below 40 and hand mules for counts above. Dobson & Barlow continued to construct hand-mules in considerable numbers throughout the 1860s but orders dropped off after 1871, the last being made in 1879. An analysis of counts for orders in 1884 and 1906, which were all for self-actors, shows how the self-actor could now be used to spin across the whole range of counts (Table 2.2). The available records for Platt Brothers of Oldham do not go so far back as for Dobson & Barlow, but they also were making hand mules up to 1877, although in smaller numbers.[15] An analysis of counts for mule orders by Platt Brothers in 1884 and 1906 reflects the fact that they were serving the Oldham coarse and medium counts trade, but still shows the range of counts then possible by self-actor mules (Table 2.3).

Table 2.1 Dobson & Barlow Ltd, mule orders against yarn count 1856
Derived from Lancashire Record Office (LRO) DDPSL/2/25/1

Count Range	Hand Mules	Self-Acting Mules
Not stated	4	1
1–20	–	–
21–40	2	14
41–60	1	–
61–80	12	1
81–100	2	–
101–120	5	–
121–140	3	–
141–160	1	–
Total	30	16

Table 2.2 Dobson & Barlow Ltd, mule orders against yarn count 1884 and 1906
Derived from LRO DDPSL/2/25/6, 7 and 11

Count Range	1884	1906
Not stated	11	4
1–20	7	5
21–40	5	4
41–60	14	9
61–80	11	17
81–100	4	11
101–120	3	4
121–140	–	7
141–160	1	4
161–180	–	–
181–200	–	2
201–220	–	2
221–240	–	2
Total	56	71

Table 2.3 Platt Brothers & Co. Ltd, mule orders against yarn count 1884 and 1906
Derived from LRO DDPSL/1/25/10, 11 and 34

Count Range	1884	1906
Not stated	10	1
1–20	48	31
21–40	62	42
41–60	29	20
61–80	5	3
81–100	–	1
101–120	–	–
121–140	–	–
141–160	1	–
Total	155	98

Table 2.4 Distribution of counts in orders for ring frames, 1890 and 1900, Platt
Brothers of Oldham (Platt) and Dobson & Barlow of Bolton (D&B)
Derived from LRO DDPSL/1/42/6–7, DDPSL/1/42/10–11, DDPSL/2/26/3
and DDPSL/2/26/4

| | 1890 | | 1900 | |
Count in range	Platt	D&B	Platt	D&B
Not Stated	5	8	6	3
1–20	42	11	46	18
21–40	74	7	60	31
41–60	1	–	13	15
61–80	1	–	5	2
81–100	–	–	3	–
Total	123	26	133	69
Of which				
Weft	12	0	25	5
Warp	111	26	108	64
Home	13	3	10	8
Export	110	23	123	61

In a lecture given to the Institution of Mechanical Engineers in 1880,
Eli Spencer of Platt Brothers implies that hand mules were still needed
for the very finest counts.[16] Although both his company and their Bolton
rivals Dobson & Barlow had ceased to make hand mules by this date, it is
possible that Richard Threlfall of Bolton, who had a reputation for building mules for the very finest counts, were still making them. However, it
is clear that the 20 years from 1880 to 1900 saw the virtual extinction of
hand mules in cotton spinning, although, according to Thomas Thornley,
some machines remained in use in Bollington in 1905 for spinning yarns
of counts up to 420.[17]

Count, however, is not the only matter of variability in yarn. For weaving different characteristics are required in warp and weft yarn. Warp yarn
was always known to spinners as 'twist', a reflection of the fact that it was
more highly twisted than weft yarn as it had to undergo greater stress both
in preparation for weaving and in the loom itself. Weft was a less heavily twisted, more open, yarn so that it could ooze out and fill the cloth,
hence being known in America as 'filling'. In addition, there were different
yarns used for other purposes like knitting, thread and lace making. All
these yarns could be produced on mules and when making weft yarn there
was the additional advantage that the mule cop could be fitted directly into
the shuttle. It should be made clear that individual mules were constructed
to produce a particular type of yarn over a particular range of counts, it was
not possible to use a given machine to produce any yarn. In weft mules

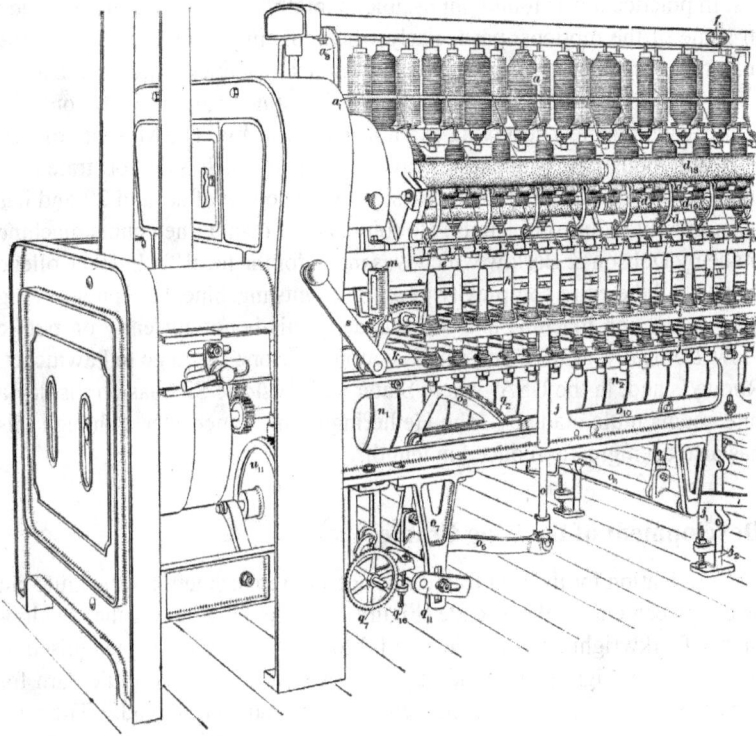

Figure 2.3 Ring Spinning Frame.

(*Source:* 'Ring Frames, Part 1', in *ICS Reference Library,* vol. *64* (London: International Correspondence Schools Ltd, 1905), fig. 1.)

the spindles were closer together than in twist mules, the standard gauges being one and one-eighth of an inch for weft and one and three-eighths of an inch for twist. Different gauges were used for other types of yarn. The mechanisms of mules for finer counts differed considerably from those used for the coarser counts.

However, in developing the self-acting mule to spin all counts and types of yarn, it had become a machine of considerable complexity (Figure 2.1). One contemporary description of the mule identifies no less than 413 individual features on a medium counts mule, a fine counts mule would have more than this, while the equivalent description for ring frames identifies only 173 features (Figure 2.3). Platt Brothers catalogued of the order of 2000 parts for their mules.[18] Despite initial hopes that it could be tended by unskilled workers this had never happened and mule minders remained skilled work-ers. In practice it was found impossible to totally avoid manual intervention in some of the motions, particularly when spinning finer counts. Also the maintenance and adjustment of these complex machines required consider-able skill. The complexity of the cotton spinning mule can now only be appreciated by a few surviving examples in museums. The Museum of Sci-ence and Industry in Manchester have a machine which is demonstrated but this is a coarse counts machine, designed for counts of around 20 and has been greatly reduced in length. Bolton Council own a fine counts machine made by Dobson & Barlow which was made for the local Technical College and has all the extra complexity of a fine counts machine, but is not as long as a production machine and unfortunately this is not currently on public view. Ironically, to see a fine counts cotton mule one has to go to Pawtucket, Rhode Island, in the USA, where Slater Mill Historic Site has on display a fine counts mule made by John Hetherington of Manchester, although this has also been greatly reduced in length.

Development of the Ring Frame

The motivation for the ring frame was not as a replacement for the mule but as a replacement for the throstle (Figure 2.5). The throstle was the develop-ment of Arkwright's water frame and throstle spun yarn was recognised as being of very high quality and in some respects superior to mule yarn for certain specialised purposes, particularly for producing thread.[19] The yarn produced was a round yarn, less woolly, and had no variation in twist. How-ever, the throstle had serious disadvantages. Because the yarn was under greater strain during spinning it was only suitable for highly twisted yarns and could not spin counts above about 36. Spindle speed was low, restricted to below 7000 rpm, as when running at higher speeds it was found that the centrifugal force caused the flyer legs to spread and even break. Also, its power consumption was high. Finally, the bobbins were small requiring frequent doffing, that is the process of removing the full bobbins and putting new empty ones onto the spindles, which was a slow and difficult operation necessitating lifting the flyers off the spindle first.

The throstle had one important advantage in that the spinning process was totally automatic; not only was human intervention not required but it was impossible. Thus, it could be tended by unskilled workers. In terms of productivity the continuous spinning system of the throstle would appear to have the advantage over the intermittent spinning system of the mule, which is not being productive for the part of the cycle when it is winding the yarn on. However, it is not as simple as this because if the throstle's spindles are running much slower than those of the mule then it could be less productive.

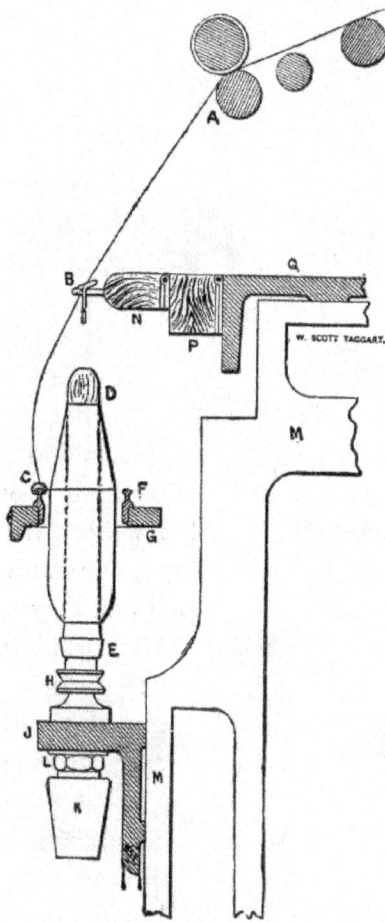

Figure 2.4 The ring spinning system. The spindle is driven and yarn spun and wound-on continuously.

(*Source:* William Scott-Taggart, *Cotton Spinning, vol. 3* (London: Macmillan & Co. Ltd, 5th edn, 1938), fig. 151.)

For example, a mule running at 9,000 rpm which is spinning for 10 seconds then winding on for 5 seconds will have an effective spindle speed of 6,000 rpm. So, a continuous spinner has to have a spindle speed in excess of 6,000 rpm to be more productive than the mule, particularly if more twist is being put in to produce yarn of the same count. The frequency and length of time taken for doffing also reduced productivity.

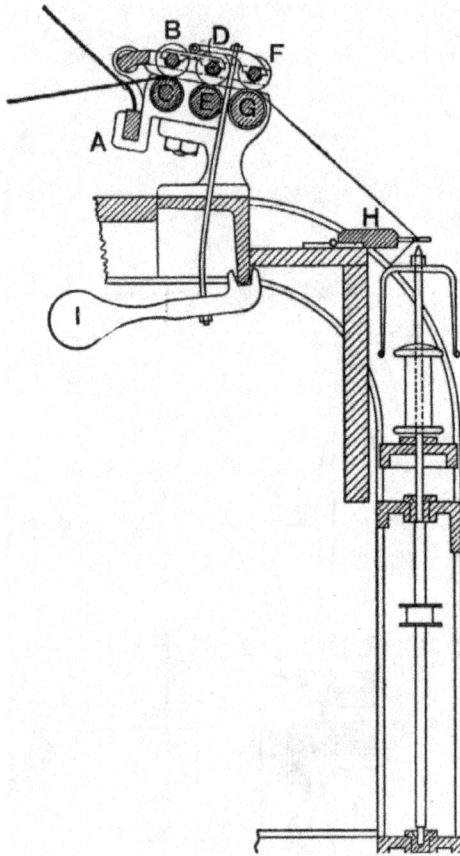

Figure 2.5 The flyer, or throstle, spinning system. The flyer is driven and yarn spun and wound-on continuously.

(*Source:* William S. Murphy (ed.), *The Textile Industries, vol. 3* (London: Gresham, 1910), fig. 136.)

Lancashire with its interest in fine counts spinning set about developing the self-acting mule to increase productivity and reduce the skilled labour content. America, on the other hand, is credited with developing the continuous spinning system and ultimately producing the ring spinning system as skilled labour was in very short supply and there was little interest in fine counts spinning. Montgomery's 1840 account of the cotton manufacture of the United States makes clear the dependence of the industry on the throstle. Virtually all warp yarn, except very fine warp yarn, was spun on the throstle and in many places weft was as well. However, elsewhere weft was mule spun.[20] Thus there was interest in America in developing self-acting mules. One example is the machine patented by Ira and Aden Gay in 1829, and a later one is that of Benjamin Lapham of 1840.[21] Ultimately, none of these were successful and it was the Roberts self-actor which came to be used in America.

Conversely, there was interest in Britain in solving the problems of throstle spinning. The diligent reader of the *Textile Manufacturer,* particularly during the 1880s when the question of ring spinning was being extensively debated, will come across claims that ring spinning was invented in England, had been taken to America and now had come back again. On investigation none of these claims stand up, but if there is any prior British claim to have invented ring spinning then it is to be found in the series of patents taken out by Archibald Thompson between 1801 and 1809. The first of these, concerned with the manufacture of ropes and cordage, describes a hemp spinning machine which has a peculiar form of flyer which he calls a 'jack'.[22] He does not describe the motivation for this design, but it is clear from what he says in his 1809 patent that he was trying to solve the problem of the legs of the flyer spreading outwards at high speeds. He says that his jack solved this problem but increased the resistance through the air. He then goes on to describe a spinning system using a ring 'On the upper side [of which] is an eye through which the yarn passes to the bobbin; and as the ring and eye turn round, the yarn receives its twist'.[23] Unfortunately there is no drawing to accompany this patent so it is difficult to see exactly what this system looked like; it seems to describe the replacing of the flyer with a complete ring, but this was driven like the flyer. So the use of the term 'ring' should not mislead into thinking this was anything like the later ring and traveller system.

But whatever the precedents, credit for the system of ring spinning is normally given to John Thorp of Providence, Rhode Island, who took out a US patent in November 1828, an English version being taken out by George William Lee in May 1829 (Figure 2.6).[24] However, it is doubtful whether this credit is justified because the system described here is not the ring and traveller system which later became known as ring spinning. There would be more justice in crediting John Thorp with the invention of the cap frame, another substitute for the flyer, credit for which is normally given to Charles Danforth. Danforth did indeed take out a US Patent for a system like the cap frame in September 1828 but a later patent by John Thorp resembles more closely what came to be known as cap spinning (Figure 2.7).[25]

The motivation for John Thorp's invention was to improve the throstle frame. He says the nature of his invention '. . . to consist in substituting for the ordinary flyer used in spinning machines a hook, which I cause

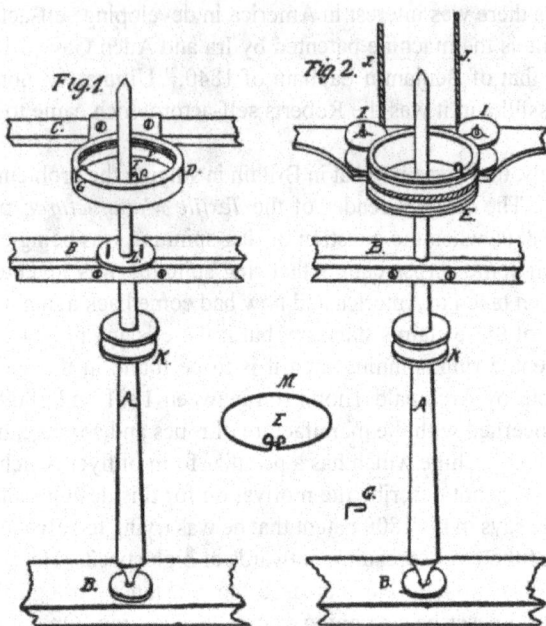

Figure 2.6 Drawings from Thorp's 1828 Spinning Patent showing his two spinning
systems. The left hand one, where the spindle is driven, most closely
resembles the later ring and traveller system. In the right hand one the
ring is driven.

(*Source:* Robert E. Naumberg, 'Two American textile pioneers', *Transactions of the Newcomen Society,* 6 (1925–6), fig. 32.)

to revolve round or with a circular rim or hoop, whereby I am enabled to
obtain a greater speed than the arms of the flyer and common operations of
the bobbin will allow of, and to increase the length of the bobbins so that
a greater quantity of yarn can be spun before they require shifting, and to
produce a more constant and even tension of the yarn than is produced in the
common mode of spinning, while the trembling of the spindle is less injuri-
ous when fitted in my manner'. He in fact shows two separate systems: in
the first the spindle is driven, in the second the spindle is stationary, while
his flyer-substitute is driven, as in the flyer frame (Figure 2.6). Both have
a rail containing holes through which the spindles protrude. In the first a
circular rim attached to the rail surrounds each spindle, on the outside of
the rim is a groove into which a ring, free to rotate, is placed. This ring has
a hook through which the yarn passes and so to the bobbin which is driven

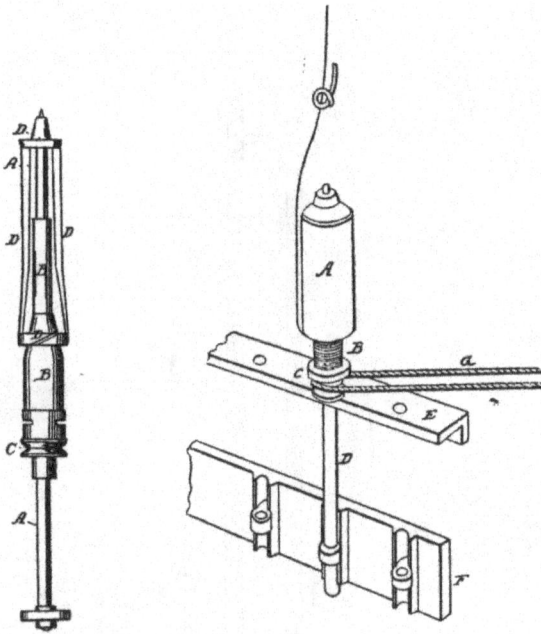

Figure 2.7 Cap Spinning Systems: Danforth's (left) and Thorp's (right).

(*Source:* Robert E. Naumberg, 'Two American textile pioneers', *Transactions of the New-comen Society,* 6 (1925–6), figs 26, 27.)

with the spindle. As the spindle is driven, the ring and its hook lags behind and so the yarn is twisted and wound on. A variation of this has a hook attached to a segment which travels in a groove cut in the top of the rim but it is difficult to interpret the description here and the drawing is unclear. What does he mean by a 'segment' and how does this segment stay in the groove? However, it is this part of the patent which seems to come closest to the ring and traveller system. In the second system the hook is cut into a circular hoop and this hoop itself is driven, the bobbin being then dragged round as in the throstle.[26]

Who exactly invented the ring and traveller system and when is not known with certainty and Thomas Navin's observation, made over 50 years ago, that the early development of ring spinning is cloaked in mystery is still true.[27] But what is certain is that the ring and traveller system first appears in England in a patent of 1834 granted to Thomas Sharp and Richard Roberts, described as being an invention communicated to them by a certain foreigner residing abroad (Figure 2.8), but it has not been possible to trace a

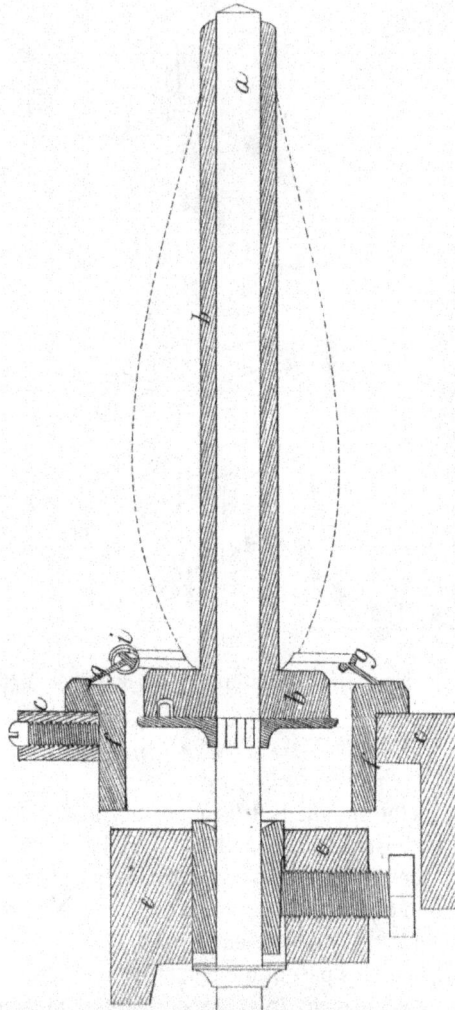

Figure 2.8 Spindle with ring and traveller from the Thomas Sharp and Richard
       Roberts patent of 1834.

(*Source:* English Patent 6690, 8/10/1834.)

US equivalent of this.[28] A study of the secondary literature comes up with
claims that it was invented in about 1830 by one variously called Jenk,
Jenks or Jencks, alternatively it is said to have been invented in 1829 by
Addison and Stevens.[29] The fact that the preamble to Sharp and Roberts'

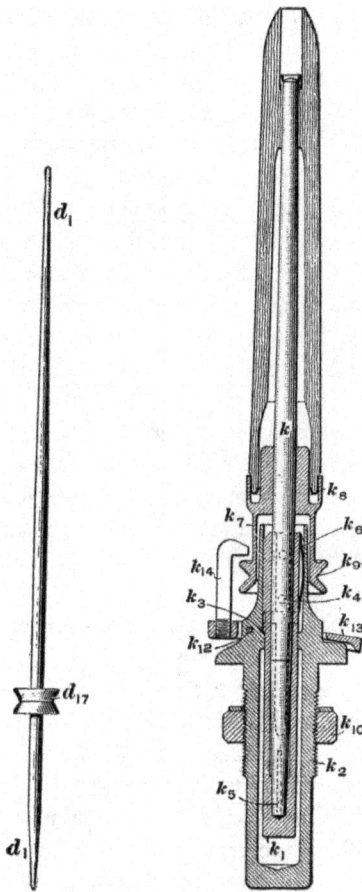

Figure 2.9 Spindles: (left) mule spindle and (right) flexible ring spindle.

(*Source:* 'Cotton Mules, Part 1', in *ICS Reference Library, vol. 64* (London: International Correspondence Schools Ltd, 1905), fig. 14; 'Ring Frames, Part 1', in *ICS Reference Library, vol. 64* (London: International Correspondence Schools Ltd, 1905), fig. 15(c).)

patent refers to 'a foreigner' in the singular would seem to favour Jenks, but this cannot be regarded as conclusive.

Again, the motivation for the Sharp and Roberts patent is improvements in throstles and three-quarters of the patent are devoted to improvements to throstle frames in general. They do not use the term traveller, but call it a 'spiral flyer' and they describe how these travellers can be made from a wire spiral. They also envisage that the ring could be driven to reduce friction between ring and traveller, thus enabling higher speeds and the spinning of finer yarns than was possible with the throstle. This system would now be referred to as a 'live ring' and has only recently returned to use in ring spinning technology. Sharp & Roberts apparently manufactured some frames which were said to produce high quality yarn, and indeed exhibited one at the Great Exhibition in 1851.[30] But it did not enter into general use as a cotton spinning frame at that time.

The early diffusion of ring spinning in both the USA and England was slow and contemporary and later commentators have invoked 'prejudice' to explain this. Evan Leigh argued that people became prejudiced against it because of the failure of the cap frame as a system for cotton spinning, although it did come to be used in worsted spinning. Evan Leigh enumerates the problems which were found with the cap system as a cotton spinner, the most serious being the undesirable characteristics of the resulting yarn. Harold Catling, whose views are to be respected as he was a textile engineer, says the reasons for the non-adoption of the cap frame are unconvincing, but the fact that it was not used even in America for cotton spinning suggests that they were genuine reasons. Indeed Montgomery, writing in 1840, maintained that the cap frame was less successful in the USA than in Great Britain.[31]

But it is evident that further development was needed before the ring and traveller became a viable spinning system which could replace the throstle. This took another two decades, even in the USA, and longer before it could replace mule. Although Montgomery says in 1840 that it was being used in several places with great satisfaction, according to Navin the first commercially successful ring frames were produced in 1845 by Fales & Jenks of Pawtucket, followed by the Whitin Machine Works who were making 50 a year by 1849.[32] The Lowell Machine Shops did not start making ring frames until after 1855 but by 1860 they were making more rings than throstles and had ceased to make throstles by 1870.[33] The Saco Water Power Company in 1848 equipped their two mills with throstles for spinning both warp and weft. However, they were dissatisfied with this machinery and 1851 the throstles for spinning weft were replaced by mules. In 1854 a third mill was built and this was equipped with ring frames. Then in 1870 all the throstles in the first two mills were replaced with ring frames, as were some of the weft mules, but the rest of the mules were replaced with new mules.[34] Copeland quotes figures of 3.7 million ring spindles and 3.4 million mule spindles in the USA in 1870 but says nothing about throstles, which are probably included in the ring spindle figure.[35] Throstles were still being used at this date since Webber quotes power tests made on throstles between 1871 and 1874.[36] Copeland's figures also show that the number of mule spindles continued to increase until 1900, although at a lower rate than ring spindles, and that it was only after 1900 that they began to decrease,

Table 2.5 Annual number of patents granted for mule spinning and ring spinning 1825–1900
Derived from the Patent Abridgements.

Year	Mule Patents	Ring Patents	Year	Mule Patents	Ring Patents
1825	4	–	1863	21	–
1826	2	–	1864	20	1
1827	1	–	1865	9	–
1828	1	–	1866	9	3
1829	–	1	1867	14	3
1830	1	–	1868	12	10
1831	1	–	1869	11	8
1832	–	–	1870	15	6
1833	3	–	1871	20	3
1834	3	1	1872	17	6
1835	1	–	1873	19	13
1836	4	–	1874	19	13
1837	1	1	1875	11	5
1838	2	–	1876	23	17
1839	3	–	1877	17	17
1840	3	–	1878	17	26
1841	1	–	1879	22	20
1842	4	–	1880	14	21
1843	1	–	1881	12	33
1844	3	–	1882	11	32
1845	5	–	1883	10	30
1846	3	–	1884	25	33
1847	6	1	1885	16	19
1848	5	–	1886	20	16
1849	7	2	1887	23	29
1850	3	2	1888	28	21
1851	1	–	1889	20	25
1852	7	–	1890	18	22
1853	20	2	1891	25	13
1854	18	1	1892	27	25
1855	20	2	1893	28	24
1856	19	1	1894	20	20
1857	13	1	1895	18	24
1858	18	1	1896	16	22
1859	19	–	1897	27	25
1860	19	2	1898	20	30
1861	23	2	1899	25	23
1862	17	1	1900	11	24

Note: Some patents apply to both rings and mules and are counted in both columns.

showing an absolute displacement of mule spindles by ring spindles. Before 1900, rings and mules should be seen as complementary rather than competing technologies.

Thus, in the USA ring spinning became a viable technology in the 1850s and the 1860s were the crucial decade when it was able to replace throstle spinning. But it is clear that the potential of ring spinning technology was recognised in the USA and efforts were made to overcome the problems, in contrast to Britain where there was little interest in the technology until the late 1860s when it had been successfully established in the USA. This is demonstrated by the number of patents granted in Britain (England before 1852) for mule spinning and ring spinning (Table 2.5). There were very few ring patents before the new patent law of 1852, but rather more mule patents. The 1852 patent law, which made it easier and cheaper to take out a patent, caused a big jump in the number of mule patents but ring patents remained at a low level until 1868, when there is a notable increase and from 1877 onwards the number of ring patents is comparable with, and often exceeds, the number of mule patents.[37]

Technical Problems in Developing Ring Spinning

A study of contemporary literature and of patents shows the considerable number of problems which needed solving before the ring frame could approach the versatility of the mule.[38] The major problems were:

1   The problem of developing a fast running spindle which would remain balanced, take the minimum amount of power and could be adequately lubricated. This was undoubtedly the key problem; the ring frame had eliminated the flyer which restricted the speed of the throstle but its speed was still limited. The yarn provided an unbalancing pull on the spindle which resulted in destructive vibrations at high speeds. Also power requirements increased and lubrication became a problem. To achieve theoretical productivity gains, speeds needed to be in excess of two-thirds of mule spindle speeds.[39]

2   The concentricity of spindle and ring. The spindle had to be exactly central in the ring.[40]

3   The build-up of loose fibres on the traveller. Fibres had a tendency to become detached from the yarn and fix themselves to the traveller, thereby increasing its weigh and adversely affecting spinning conditions.[41]

4   Materials for rings and travellers. The considerable friction between the ring and the traveller was another limitation on speed. The traveller was a particular problem because it was a very small object travelling at high speed with a small heat capacity so frictional heating could cause the metal to soften and to distort. High speeds could also lead

to rapid wear of both ring and traveller. A related problem was that of producing the rings, these need to have a totally smooth surface.[42]

5   Shape of travellers. The traveller is a very small object, but its exact shape is crucial to successful spinning and also affects the amount of frictional heat generated. The traveller described in the 1834 Sharp and Roberts patent would probably not have been very successful.

6   Ballooning. The yarn being twisted between the eye above the spindle and the traveller (B and C in Figure 2.4) balloons outwards. This is another factor limiting speed because if the balloons on adjacent spindles become too large they will collide resulting in yarn breakage.[43]

7   Doffing, that is removing the full bobbins of yarn and replacing them with empty ones. Although simpler than in the throstle this was a more difficult job than in the mule, particularly if the yarn had to be re-threaded through the travellers.[44]

8   Amount of twist. Because the yarn was under greater tension, in order to prevent breakage a greater amount of twist had to be put in than would be put in when spinning the same counts of yarn on a mule. The resulting yarn was therefore harder than mule spun yarn resulting in cloth produced from ring yarn having a different 'handle' to that produced from mule yarn.

9   Variation of twist. It can be shown mathematically that for constant spindle speed and rate of yarn delivery, the amount of twist in the yarn varies as the bobbin fills. This issue was hotly debated at the time but the amount of variation is in fact very small, less than 2%. But it is true that even small cyclic variations in yarn can show up in undesirable ways in finished cloth.

10 Cotton quality. Again largely because of the tension the yarn is under when being spun, higher grade cotton was needed for spinning on ring frames, particularly as regards to uniformity of staple length. The mule could cope with much greater variability in cotton quality.

11 Quality of preparation. This is related to cotton quality, but any unevenness in the rovings would pass straight through the ring spinning system and appear in the finished yarn, in contrast to mule spinning which tended to even out these variations.

12 The production of weft. This was problematic because weft required less twist than warp yarns and was required in cop form either spun on the bare spindle, as in mules, or on small pirns rather than large bobbins.[45]

All these issues cannot be dealt with in any detail here but it is undoubtedly the satisfactory solution to the first of these which resulted in a great leap forward for the ring frame in the 1870s. The great importance attached to this advance in the United States is indicted by the large amount of litigation it produced concerning patents. J. H. Sawyer of Lowell, Massachusetts, took out a US patent for a new design of spindle on 11 April 1871, although previous to this he had sold rights to George Draper & Son of Hopedale, Massachusetts. The British version of the patent predates the US version by almost a month and was taken out by John B. Booth of Preston and is said to be in part a communication from the Draper's. Booth's patent does contain material which is not in the US patent and the spindle became known in Britain as the Booth-Sawyer spindle.[46] The importance of this advance is shown by some statistics arising from tests made in the USA which are quoted by Evan Leigh.[47] These show the number of spindles which it was found could be driven per horse power at 5,000 revolutions per minute when spinning 38's yarn:

Throstle	61
Common Ring	121
Sawyer's Ring	211
Mule	234

This shows that before the introduction of Sawyer's spindle the ring frame required almost double the power required by a mule to drive the same number of spindles, the throstle requiring twice as much again. This was a factor which would have weighed heavily against the ring frame in Lancashire. But with Sawyer's spindle the ring frame had almost caught up with the mule. The Booth-Sawyer spindle had only a short life as the next advance, by Francis Rabbeth of Pawtucket, Rhode Island, followed shortly afterwards and was introduced into Britain in about 1874 by Howard & Bullough of Accrington.[48] This was well on the way to the final solution to the problem which came in the form of the flexible spindle. No one name appears to be associated with this development, but Platt Brothers first used flexible spindles in 1886 and they rapidly superseded the Rabbeth spindle.[49] The alternative names of 'self-centring' or 'top' spindle describes the principle of this spindle in that, rather than being held rigidly in bearings, the spindle was allowed to float and find its own centre, rather like a spinning top. The resulting spindle was quite complex and this was one area in which ring frames were more complex than mules (Figure 2.9). However, over a century later the same principle is still used in ring frame spindles.

But it should be noted that power requirements for ring spinning still remained an issue and figures published later do not give such close agreement as those quoted above, which were no doubt obtained under ideal experimental conditions. Although not in a format which allows direct comparison, Platt Brothers' catalogue of 1929 gives the following data for spindles per horse power:[50]

Twist mule	9,600rpm	115 spindles
Weft mule	9,600rpm	175 spindles
Warp ring frame	6,000rpm	120 spindles
Warp ring frame	7,000rpm	100 spindles
Warp ring frame	8,000rpm	90 spindles
Warp ring frame	8,500rpm	80 spindles
Warp ring frame	9,000rpm	70 spindles

The other serious problem in ring frame development was the spinning of weft yarns. Writing in 1884, Richard Marsden claimed that although a considerable amount of weft was spun on ring frames in the USA, it was done so uneconomically and in Britain only Samuel Brooks of Manchester had paid much attention to the problem, having produced a satisfactory frame which had sold mainly on the Continent.[51] The problem of spinning weft yarn was that it was more lightly twisted, and therefore weaker, than twist yarn. Also it was required in cop form, wound on the bare spindle or small diameter tapered bobbins called pirns, which could be placed in a shuttle, rather than the large diameter straight bobbins which were suitable for other yarn. But this was found very difficult to perform because when winding on small diameters the tension in the yarn increases, in fact it tends to infinity as the spindle diameter tends to zero, leading it to break. This problem was recognised very early in the development of ring spinning and a patent by Bodmer of 1837 presents a means of trying to solve this problem.[52] A very considerable amount of effort was expended during the nineteenth century to try and develop a bare-spindle ring spinning frame. In fact it became something of a search for the 'holy grail' which attracted the attention of persons who were not themselves involved in the design of textile machinery such as the partners of Stott & Sons the mill architects.[53] In this and other cases experimental machines were constructed but despite enthusiastic press reports about the quality of spinning done on these machines when demonstrated it was not possible to produce satisfactory results in every day operation. The only design to have achieved any measure of success was that patented by Perkins, Wimpenny and Evans in 1882, the concept employed being very similar to that in Bodmer's 1837 patent (Figure 2.10).[54] Platt Brothers of Oldham acquired the rights to this patent and made 666 machines with a total of 238 304 spindles between 1885 and 1900.[55] All but 34 of these machines were for export, and 30 of these home machines were for Lister & Co. of Bradford for silk, not cotton, spinning. But elsewhere the prospect of being able to spin weft on a ring frame, thus avoiding the skills necessary to operate mules, was clearly an attractive prospect. A total of 394

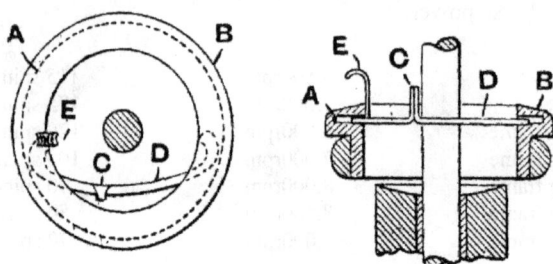

Figure 2.10 Perkins, Wimpenny and Evans modified ring and traveller spinning
system for weft yarns (British Patent 2838, 16/6/1882).

(*Source:* Joseph Nasmith, *Modern Cotton Spinning Machinery* (Manchester: John Heywood,
1890), figures 200, 201.)

of these machines were sold to mills in Russia via their agents De Jersey
& Co., while Poznanski in Lodz, Poland, purchased 131 machines. Other
mills in Lodz also purchased these machines, but not all found them satisfactory: Heinzel & Kumitzer purchased a single machine in 1893 which
was described as a 'Trial order to decide whether mules or ring frames
should be adopted,' but they ordered no more so the trial must have been
unsatisfactory.[56]

Ultimately, the effort to spin weft on the bare spindle was abandoned
and the ring frame mechanism was developed by the 1890s to spin weft
yarn on pirns, using small diameter rings to minimise yarn tension. Platt
Brothers quoted ring diameters of one and one-eighth of an inch to one
and three-eighths of an inch for weft and one and three-eighths of an inch
to two and a quarter inches for warp. Different spindles were needed to
carry pirns and bobbins. In both cases paper tubes could be used instead
of wooden bobbins, requiring yet a different spindle design.[57] American
machine makers similarly developed ring frames to spin weft (filling) on
pirns and the Northrop automatic loom was designed to take weft wound on
pirns.[58] Nasmith writing in 1890 describes a frame by Howard & Bullough
which is to this design and their advertisement in the same volume states
that these frames can compete with mules in spinning weft.[59] Table 2.4
shows how orders to both Platt Brothers and Dobson & Barlow for weft
frames increased between 1890 and 1900. These figures include the Perkins, Wimpenny & Evans patent frames made by Platt Brothers. However,
weft frames remained in a minority as in both years under 20% of all ring
frames constructed were for weft showing the ring spun weft was not as
widely acceptable as ring spun warp yarn. Except for one weft frame made

in 1900 by Dobson & Barlow, in both years all the weft frames constructed were for export. The take up of weft ring frames in Britain remained low and as late as 1947 only 5.5% of ring frames installed in Britain had ring diameters of one and three-eighths of an inch or less and therefore suitable for weft.[60] Table 2.4 also demonstrates that during the 1890s progress was made into spinning higher counts on ring frames, both Platt Brothers and Dobson & Barlow showing increased orders by 1900 for counts over 40s.[61] This shows that the Lancashire machine makers were actively developing the ring frame to extend its range.

The Introduction of Ring Spinning in Lancashire

The championing of ring spinning in Britain has often been credited to two newer firms, Samuel Brooks, later Brooks & Doxey, of Manchester and Howard & Bullough of Accrington, rather than the old established firms like Platt Brothers of Oldham or Dobson & Barlow of Bolton.[62] However, Platt Brothers were interested in ring spinning at an early date as by 1864 they were producing, in small numbers, ring and traveller machines for woollen doubling.[63] They made their first cotton ring spinning frames in 1867 for export to Harmony Mills, Cohoes, New York after engaging in industrial espionage. Robert Johnson, the manager of Harmony Mills, sent them a dismantled American-made frame and asked them to copy it. The entry in the order book is dated 13 March 1867 and a portion of the covering letter copied into the order book reads: 'I am sending boxes containing 1 spinning frame of 160 spindles same as I want you to build for us, send sample frame as soon as possible. This frame is one of the best style and make in the country, and the nearer you can make to this one the better it will take into the American market.' Despite having never built a cotton ring spinning frame before, they evidently constructed one with considerable rapidity and to Robert Johnson's satisfaction as a further 6 were ordered in August 1867, then another 52 the following month and 10 in April next year. During this period they also constructed cotton spinning ring frames for Gordon & MacKay in Toronto, Canada, and for the Kolbermoor Spinnerie in Germany. However, it was not until October 1877 that they first made a machine for the home market, for J. B. Wood of Middleton.[64]

The fact that they acquired the technology by espionage, which they would not want to be made known, and the ten year delay before supplying a machine for the home market, no doubt explains why contemporaries seem to have been unaware of Platt's early involvement in ring spinning. Nasmith, for example, in his seemingly comprehensive account of the introduction of the ring frame in Britain, makes no mention of Platt Brothers. He states that the ring and traveller came to be used as a system for doubling before it was used for spinning, and claims that in 1866 J. & P. Coats and Clark & Co., both of Paisley and having mills in America, introduced frames from America for doubling and subsequently ordered frames for this purpose from McGregor of Manchester. He credits McGregor with making the first ring spinning frame in June 1867 for Knowles of Burnley and for the first large installation in Britain of fourteen frames at John Dugdale of Burnley in October 1869. Samuel Brooks did not begin to build ring frames until 1872 after they had sent a representative, James Blakey, to America to investigate the technology.[65] The fact that they and Howard & Bullough then went on to become known as the major constructors of ring frames suggests that Platt's piece of espionage did not do them much good. Dobson & Barlow, Platt's rival in Bolton, did not make their first ring frame until 1873 and this was for export.[66]

By the 1870s, throstle spindles were very much in a minority in Lancashire, but were still used to produce the specialised yarns to which they were suited. Throstle spinners survived in areas which were somewhat peripheral to the main cotton industry such as Rochdale, Todmorden and Wigan. Given the origin of the ring frame as an alternative to the throstle, it is not surprising that these companies rapidly adopted ring spinning. Dobson & Barlow made their last throstles in 1888, Platt Brothers their last in 1890.[67] By 1911 Worrall's Directory for Lancashire listed only seven firms involved in throstle spinning.[68] An example of this is Fieldens at Todmorden, who have been presented by J. S. Toms as innovators in both ring spinning and automatic weaving. In 1856 two-thirds of their spindles were throstles, the sort of proportion that would be found in New England. They continued to purchase new throstles until 1885, when they moved over to ring frames and in the 1890s began spinning weft on ring frames. They were an integrated spinning and weaving firm, but little information is available on the nature of their output, although a 1912 photograph of the interior of one of their weaving sheds shows only plain cloths being woven.[69] New ring spinning mills also began to be built from the 1880s onwards, and an examination of entries for these in annual editions of Worrall's Textile Directory for Lancashire shows that they tended to produce specialised types of yarn, often for purposes other than weaving. These uses included knitting, thread making and rope yarns, but where ring mills were producing yarns for weaving it was often for specialised cloths such as crepes which required hard twisted doubled yarns for warps. Thus, the notable group of Rochdale ring spinning companies, whose financial performance has been compared favourably with mule spinning companies by J. S. Toms, all included doubling capacity.[70] Another example is the Nile Mill in Oldham, a large ring spinning mill built in 1898 which contained 94,000 ring spindles and 14,000 doubling spindles, for producing, amongst other things, sewing, crochet, fish net, heald, mercerising, lace and curtain yarns.[71] From this it may be concluded that Lancashire was not backward in using ring spindles for purposes to which they were particularly suited.

However, for the vast majority of weaving purposes, ring yarn was considered to be inferior to mule spun. Cloth woven from such yarns was considered to have a 'raw' appearance and lacked the qualities of cloth made from mule spun yarns. Mule spun yarn had greater elasticity, ooziness, fullness and regularity, and thus provided better 'cover' and appearance to the cloth.[72] 'S.E.B.' writing in the *Textile Manufacturer* in 1889, after describing the ring frame as a replacement for the throstle, notes that there were then a variety of opinions as to whether and as to what extent the ring frame could replace the mule.[73] His personal view was that, as twisting and winding took place simultaneously in the ring frame, it could never replace the mule, unless the finer yarns were to go out of use. An editorial of nearly two decades later in the *Textile Manufacturer* referred to similar issues, although concluded that the quality of ring spun yarn was improving.[74] Technical factors such as these were clearly of major importance in retaining mule spinning in Lancashire. We do not propose to go here into the related issue of automatic weaving, but in passing it should be noted that because of its mechanical construction, ring spun yarn was stronger than mule spun yarn and this was important for Northrop automatic looms where the weft was under considerable tension when being threaded into the shuttle and yarn breakage rates had to be kept down in order to achieve worthwhile productivity gains. But the resulting cloth would lack the qualities of cloth from mule spun yarn.

The Triumph of Ring Spinning in the Twentieth Century

Thomas Thornley was Spinning Master at the Technical College in Bolton who compiled, amongst other things, two massive treatises on the self-acting mule. He clearly revelled in the complexity of the machine and held the ring frame in contempt. In the preface to the third edition of the first volume of this work written in 1906, he states:

> No machine in existence is more highly developed, more subject to study and investigation, or more expertly handled than the self-acting mule of one make or another. It is a machine which finds good work for intelligent, hard-working men, whereas the ring frame is attended by women, so that the continued progress of this splendid and useful machine is to be welcomed on this account.

He concludes this volume with a description of the mule made by Howard & Bullough of Accrington, noting with pleasure that this firm who had long championed the ring frame had recently succumbed to market pressures and started producing mules. However, 20 years later he may have been having doubts. In the third edition of his *Advanced Cotton Spinning* published in 1923, he actually places the chapter on ring spinning before that on mule spinning and, while repeating in a rather muted form sentiments similar to those quoted above, he does admit that there are now in Britain many successful ring spinning concerns. However, other textile engineers were more outspoken. Writing five years later, Lawrence Balls, who ran the Fine Cotton Spinners and Doublers research laboratory at Bollington, had this to say:

> [The mule] had been described and discussed in the text-books until one had an uneasy feeling that it was a mechanical monstrosity, entitled to reverence as one of the most ingenious of all machines, and yet impracticable by any ordinary standards of judgement. If we may imagine the record of invention rolled up, so that the men of to-day could be confronted with the modern mule as a new invention, I have not the least doubt that the inventor would be unable to sell a machine to any spinner; the size, cost, complication, slowness and the peak-load power demand would separately and collectively outweigh any claim or any demonstration concerning the quality of its product. The mule seems to stand in the same relation to us of to-day as does a Dinosaur.

Nine years later when Allan Ormerod joined the reputedly progressive firm of Ashtons of Hyde he was surprised to find them still using mules, although was reassured to discover that they were only used to produce the highly specialised yarn needed for vacuum cleaner bags. When in 1944 Platt Brothers produced a book on *Modern Cotton Spinning and Doubling Machinery* to encourage re-equipment after the war, it made no mention of mule spinning; the textile engineers had finally been won over to the ring frame.[75]

In the second half of the twentieth century the majority of the world's yarn was spun on ring frames, although the ring frame is still limited to counts below about 160, the higher counts which were spun on mules are no longer spun.[76] So, 'S.E.B.' was incorrect in his 1889 prediction that if the mule was supplanted by the ring, then the finer yarns would go out of use. But the ring frame has not remained unchallenged and current spindle speeds of around 25,000 rpm are considered to be as high as technically feasible. The biggest challenger is the open-end, or rotor, spinning system which can produce yarn at a rate of up to ten times that of a ring spindle.

But it has not made the inroads into ring spinning which might be expected from this productivity increase because the resulting yarn has a different, and less desirable, structure to ring yarn and the system has been found most suitable for yarns of counts under 40, a situation remarkably parallel to that between the ring and mule a century earlier. However, these problems are being overcome and the number of rotors in the world increased by 1.2% in 2001 compared with a decrease of 6% in the number of ring spindles, China taking a particular interest in this technology.[77]

Conclusion

This paper has demonstrated that, although the basic concept of ring spinning originated in the 1830s as a development of the throstle, it was not fully usable as there were inherent problems with the technology, viable solutions for which did not emerge until the 1860s and after. Weft spinning was particularly problematic and it was not until the 1890s that satisfactory weft spinning ring frames were developed, after a lot of effort had been expended on alternative continuous spinning systems. This contrasted with mule spinning where, given a skilled operator, any type and count of yarn could be spun. The problem in mule spinning was to automate this process and although the basic solution to this problem was available in 1830, it was not until the 1870s that the self-acting mule became a viable machine for the finer yarn counts. But in doing so the mule became a machine of considerable complexity which still required skilled labour to operate. By contrast the developments in the ring frame retained its basic simplicity and operation by unskilled labour. By 1900 the ring frame was capable of spinning counts below 40s and above this for warp yarns. The resulting yarn had different characteristics to mule spun yarn, which was a particular problem when used for weft. The continuing development of ring spinning in the twentieth century meant, however, the mule ceased to be a viable machine irrespective of the quality of yarn produced.

So what does this understanding of the technological development of ring spinning have to contribute to the classic 'rings versus mules' debate? The contribution can only be a modest one, no claims can be made to have finally resolved the debate, nor can we make any direct contribution to those aspects of the debate which ultimately concern whether neo-classical or other economic theory is adequate for explaining Lancashire's decline. However, there are three points which can be made. The first two are related: first, it is wrong to regard the American cotton spinning industry during this period as technically more advanced than the Lancashire industry; and second, the technology developed by Lancashire was able to produce a wider range of yarns than the American technology. The key fact behind both these points is that the ring frame was developed as an alternative not to the mule but to the throstle frame and this has not been adequately appreciated by previous writers, who have only mentioned the throstle in passing if at all.[78] Copeland's figures showing that 52% of spindles in America in 1870 were rings and only 48% were mules has been quoted as implying that even by this date rings were replacing mules.[79] But this is misleading as these ring spindles would have largely replaced throstles and it is doubtful whether the proportion of mule spindles in the United States had ever exceeded 50%. This should not be taken as indicating any technological superiority of the American industry since it could only spin a restricted range of coarse yarns while Lancashire had developed its technology to spin a wide range of yarns from a wide range of cottons. In this respect the Lancashire industry was technically more advanced throughout the nineteenth century and was not lagging behind. Moreover, in Lancashire the ring frame did rapidly replace the remaining throstles and was taken up for spinning yarns, often for purposes other than weaving, for which it was particularly suited. Although J. S. Toms in his comparisons of the financial performance of ring and mule spinning concerns is aware of these alternative uses and the inclusion of doubling capacity in the Rochdale ring spinning concerns studied, he does not explore the implications of this on validity of the comparisons he is making. The specialised production of these concerns no doubt explains why they remained small and were not widely emulated.[80]

The third point is that the technical considerations of yarn and cloth quality clearly influenced the choice of spinning system in Lancashire, mule yarn being seen as superior. Lazonick has argued that it was the structure of industrial organization, which imposed extra costs involved in shipping ring yarn between the spinning and weaving mills, which prevented the wider adoption of ring spinning in Lancashire.[81] Transport costs clearly were an issue, but it is wrong to see this as the sole reason. Sandberg did discuss the question of yarn quality and treated the assertions of superior quality of mule spun yarn to some scepticism.[82] In issues of quality perception is perhaps more important than reality, but we have shown here that the perception of mule spun yarn being generally superior was based on valid technological factors. The fact that the throstle spinners were willing to replace their throstles with rings, although admittedly there were no organizational issues here, shows that the Lancashire spinners were willing to move over to clearly superior technology. Another example of this would be the replacement of 'roller-and-clearer' type carding engines by the 'revolving-flat' type from the mid-1880s onwards with examples of mills replacing machinery which was not life-expired by the standards of the industry.[83] Admittedly, there were again no organizational issues involved here. Lazonick seems to turn on its head the question of the use of shorter staple cottons in Lancashire for producing yarn of the same count, again giving an erroneous impression of the Lancastrian inferiority.[84] He may be right that Lancashire spinners used shorter staple cotton to drive down the costs of mule yarn, but conversely it could be argued that one reason the mule was a superior technology for Lancashire conditions was that Lancashire had no alternative but to use a wide variety of cottons. A similar situation is noted by Glyn Jones in respect of the roller milling of wheat; Britain developed different systems of roller milling to America and other countries because it had to take wheat from a wider range of sources, it was not an inferior system to the American system which was designed to process a much narrower range of wheats.[85]

In the twentieth century the cotton industry in New England, despite using ring spinning in integrated mills, failed as profoundly as the industry in Lancashire. Laurence Gross draws a picture of decline and obsolescence at the Boott Mills in Lowell which is as grim as anything in Lancashire, while the effects of the collapse of the great Amoskeag Mills in 1936 were still felt in Manchester, New Hampshire, four decades later when Tamara Hareven and Randolph Langenbach produced their outstanding oral and pictorial study.[86] Fall River may have used more ring spindles than Oldham, but a walk round these towns today will reveal the fact that the surviving mill buildings which still form an impressive feature of the landscape have been turned to other uses or fallen derelict.[87] This suggests that there are many paths to industrial obsolescence and that the 'rings versus mules' debate has not only been given too much weight in explaining the decline of the Lancashire cotton industry, but has played too dominant a role in it's historiography.

Notes

1 William Mass and William Lazonick, 'The British Cotton Industry and International Competitive Advantage: The state of the debates', *Business History,* 32, 4 (October 1990), pp. 9–65. Andrew Marrison, 'Indian Summer, 1870–1914', in Mary B. Rose (ed.), *The Lancashire Cotton Industry: A History since 1700* Preston: Lancashire County Books, (1996), pp. 238–264.

2 J.S. Toms, 'Growth, Profits and Technological Choice: The case of the Lancashire cotton textile industry', *Journal of Industrial History,* 1 (1998), pp. 35–55. Stephen Broadberry and Andrew Marrison, 'External Economies of Scale in the Lancashire Cotton Industry, 1900–1950', *Economic History Review,* 55 (2002), pp. 51–77.

3 Oddly, by comparison there appears to have been less analysis or debate about the decline of the New England cotton industry, but see Laurence F. Gross, *The Course of Industrial Decline: The Boott Cotton Mills of Lowell, Massachusetts, 1835–1955* (Baltimore and London: John Hopkins University Press, 1993).

4 Sheila A. Mason, *Nottingham Lace 1760s-1950s* (Ilkeston: The author, 1994), p. xv.

5 Colum Giles and Ian H. Goodall, *Yorkshire Textile Mills 1770–1930* (London: HMSO, 1992). Mike Williams with D. A. Farnie, *Cotton Mills in Greater Manchester* (Preston: Carnegie, 1992). Anthony Calladine and Jean Fricker, *East Cheshire Textile Mills* (London: RCHME, 1993). Roger N. Holden, *Stott & Sons: Architects of the Lancashire Cotton Mill* (Lancaster: Carnegie, 1998).

6 Richard Hills, *Power in the Industrial Revolution* (Manchester: Manchester University Press, 1970).

7 W. English, *The Textile Industries* (London: Longmans, 1969).

8 Harold Catling, *The Spinning Mule* (Newton Abbot: David & Charles, 1970).

9 Alfred Seymour-Jones, 'The Invention of Roller Drawing in Cotton Spinning', *Transactions of the Newcomen Society,* 1 (1920–21), pp. 50–64. Robert E. Naumberg, 'Two American Textile Pioneers', *Transactions of the Newcomen Society,* 6 (1925–26), pp. 149–58. Frank Nasmith, 'Fathers of Cotton Manufacture', *Transactions of the Newcomen Society,* 6 (1925–26), pp. 159–68. H. W. Dickinson, 'Richard Roberts, his Life and Inventions', *Transactions of the Newcomen Society,* 25 (1945–47), pp. 123–37. William A. Hunter, 'James Hargraves [*sic*] and the Invention of the Spinning Jenny', *Transactions of the Newcomen Society,* 28 (1951–53), pp. 141–51. W. H. Chaloner, 'New Light on Richard Roberts, Textile Engineer (1789–1864)', *Transactions of the Newcomen Society,* 41 (1968–69), pp. 27–44. Christopher Aspin, 'New Evidence on James Hargreaves and the Spinning Jenny', *Textile History,* 1 (1968–70), pp. 119–21. K. G. Ponting, 'The Textile Inventions of Sebastian Ziani de Ferranti', *Textile History,* 4 (1973), pp. 47–67. W. English, 'A Technical Assessment of Lewis Paul's Spinning Machine', *Textile History,* 4 (1973), pp. 68–83. J. A. Iredale and P. A. Townhill, 'Silk Spinning in England: The end of an epoch', *Textile History,* 4 (1973), pp. 100–8. Harold Catling, 'The Development of the Spinning Mule', *Textile History,* 9 (1978), pp. 35–57. R. L. Hills, 'Hargreaves, Arkwright and Crompton. Why three inventors?', *Textile History,* 10 (1979), pp. 114–26.

10 English Patent No. 1879, 15/5/1792.

11 English Patent No's. 5138, 29/3/1825 and 5949, 1/7/1830.

12 For example by W. Eaton (English Patent No. 4272, 18/6/1818), J. Heathcoat (English Patent No. 4926, 20/3/1824) and M. DeJongh (English Patent No's. 5432 18/12/1826 and 5576 4/12/1827).

13 Lancashire Record Office (hearafter, LRO), Platt-Saco-Lowell Archive, Dobson & Barlow Ltd, Mule Order Books, DDPSL/2/35.

14 Textile machinery production is usually measured in numbers of spindles but unfortunately in Dobson & Barlow's Production Books the number of spindles is not always stated and occasionally not even the number of machines is given, this is particularly the case for earlier years, including 1856. So number of orders has been used which clearly shows the trend being demonstrated. Counts of yarn to be spun is not always given and where a range is given the mid-point has been taken.

15 LRO, Platt-Saco-Lowell Archive, Platt Brothers & Co. Ltd, Mule Production Books DDPSL/1/25, Mule Headstock Books DDPSL/1/36.

16 Eli Spencer, 'On Recent Improvements in the Machinery for Preparing and Spinning Cotton', *Proceedings of the Institution of Mechanical Engineers* (1880), pp. 492–528.

17 Thomas Thornley *Self-Acting Mules, vol. 1* (Manchester: John Heywood, 3rd edn, 1906), pp. 629–30. One of these machines was acquired for the Chadwick Museum in Bolton but regrettably has since been lost.

18 'Cotton Mules' and 'Ring Frames' in *ICS Reference Library, vol. 64* (London: International Correspondence Schools Ltd, 1905). Platt Brothers & Co. Ltd, *Catalogue of Details of Self-Acting Mules for Spinning Cotton and Worsted Yarns* (Oldham: Platt Brothers & Co. Ltd, 1930). The word 'feature', rather than 'parts' is used advisedly because some of these features, e.g. the spindles, were multiplied many times, while in other cases a single part, e.g. a cam, can have more than one feature identified on it. Note that some of the parts in the Platt Brothers catalogue are applicable only to worsted mules.

19 Evan Leigh, *The Science of Modern Cotton Spinning* (Manchester: A. Ireland & Co., 1871–2), p. 219. Richard Marsden, *Cotton Spinning* (London: George Bell & Sons, 1884), pp. 291–296. John Lister, *Cotton Manufacture* (London: Crosby, Lockwood & Son, 1894), pp. 72–3.

20 James Montgomery, *Cotton Manufacture of the United States of America* (Glasgow: James Niven, 1840), pp. 69–70.

21 David J. Jeremy, *Transatlantic Industrial Revolution* (Oxford: Blackwell, 1981), p. 334 (note 9). Although the Gay's sent a copy of their specification to England before it was patented in the USA, no patent was ever taken out in England. However, a copy of the specification survives in the Fielden Archives (Calderdale Archives Service, FLD620). Lapham's patent is USA Patent No. 1797 25/9/1840.

22 English Patent No. 2553, 10 November 1801.

23 English Patent No. 3202, 7 February 1809. There are also two other patents by Archibald Thomson: No. 3014, 20 February 1807, and No. 3024, 2 April 1807. 3014 has no specification enrolled and, as it had the same title as 3024, it may well be a bureaucratic error, 3024 being originally intended as the specification for 3014. Nothing seems to be known about Archibald Thomson, who describes himself as an 'engineer' residing in London in 1801 and 1807, Manchester in 1809. Confusion is caused by his name being incorrectly spelt in various places as 'Thompson' with a 'p'. English (*Textile Industry*, p. 156) refers solely to the hackling machine described in the 1801 patent. The entry in the *Biographical Dictionary of the History of Technology* (London: Routledge, 1996), p. 701, adds nothing to this and simply seems to be repeated from English even to the extent of misspelling his name and quoting the wrong number for the 1801 patent, other aspects of this patent and the other patents are not mentioned. Jeremy (*Transatlantic Industrial Revolution*, p. 214) mentions the 1809 patent in passing but his suggestion that it was not taken up because of the industry's shift to mule spinning seems unlikely, it is more likely that it was simply not a viable spinning system.

24 USA Patent X5280 20/11/1829. English Patent 5787 2/5/1829.

25 USA Patents 5214X 2/9/1828 and 5279X 25/11/1828. Naumberg, 'Two American Textile Pioneers', pp. 149–158. Jeremy (*Transatlantic Industrial Revolution*, p. 243) suggests that English Patent No. 5822 13/7/1829 to John Hutchison of Liverpool is the English version of Danforth's patent but this is somewhat doubtful, it does show a similar spinning system but is of a different form to either Danforth's or Thorp's and is not described as being a communication from abroad.

26 The wording here is taken from Lee's English version of the patent. Note that there is a later patent by John Thorp, US Patent 3766 27/9/1844, which does refer to the ring and traveller system.

27 Thomas R. Navin, *The Whitin Machine Works Since 1831* (Cambridge, MA: Harvard University Press, 1950), p. 34.

28 Patent No. 6690, 8 October 1834. Unfortunately, Richard Hills has recently confused matters by stating that this is the English version of Thorp's patent: Richard L. Hills, *Life and Inventions of Richard Roberts 1789–1864* (Ashbourne: Landmark Publishing, 2002), p. 156. Note also that this patent is missing from the Patent Abridgements on Spinning, which probably explains why it appears to have been missed by previous researchers.

29 For Jenk see W. Klein, *Manual of Textile Technology Short-staple Spinning Series, vol. 4: A Practical Guide to Ring Spinning* (Manchester: The Textile Institute, 1987), p. 1. For Jenks see M.T. Copeland, *The Cotton Manufacturing Industry of the United States* (New York: Augustus M. Kelley, 2nd edn, 1966), p. 9 who in turn quotes T. Kettle (ed.), *Eighty Years' Progress, vol. 2* (New York, 1864), p. 286. For Jencks see Leigh, *Science of Modern Cotton Spinning*, p. 224. For Addison and Stevens see Joseph Nasmith, *Modern Cotton Spinning Machinery* (Manchester: John Heywood, 1890), p. 239. Evidently copying from Nasmith in quoting Addison and Stevens is Catling, *Spinning Mule*, p. 184.

30 Hills, *Richard Roberts*, p. 156.

31 Leigh, *Modern Cotton Spinning*, pp. 208–10. Catling, *Spinning Mule*, p. 183. James Montgomery, *Cotton Manufacture of the United States of America* (Glasgow: James Niven, 1840), p. 70.

32 Navin, *Whitin Machine Works*, p. 35.

33 George Sweet Gibb, *The Saco-Lowell Shops* (Cambridge, MA: Harvard University Press, 1950), pp. 192, 649, 757.

34 Evelyn H. Knowlton, *Pepperell's Progress* (Cambridge, MA: Harvard University Press, 1948), p. 53–58, 134–138.

35 Copeland, *Cotton Manufacturing Industry of the United States*, p. 70.

36 Samuel Webber, *Manual of Power* (New York: D. Appleton & Co., 2nd edn, 1879), pp. 28, 79–80.

37 Note that some patents will apply to both mules and rings and will be counted under both headings. This is the case for patents which apply to common parts, particularly drafting rollers.

38 Leigh, *Modern Cotton Spinning*, pp. 223–35. Marsden, *Cotton Spinning*, pp. 296–314. Lister, *Cotton Manufacture*, pp. 73–81. Nasmith, *Modern Cotton Spinning Machinery*, pp. 234–59. William Scott-Taggart, *Cotton Spinning, vol. 3* (London: Macmillan & Co. Ltd, 5th edn, 1938), pp. 278–336.

39 For example, British patents: 737 18/3/1871, 2933 4/10/1872, 18 1/1/1873, 398 31/1/1874, 1835 23/5/1874, 2497 16/7/1874, 2826 24/7/1877, 807 27/2/1878, 972 11/3/1878, 1401 8/4/1878, 2872 18/7/1878.

40 For example, British patents: 166 15/1/1873, 4908 1/12/1878.

41 For example, British patents: 1610 20/4/1878, 3130 23/6/1883, 12630 20/9/1884.

42 For example, British patents: 2410 5/10/1860, 407 9/2/1866, 378 4/2/1868, 1173 25/3/1878, 1765 5/5/1879, 2549 25/6/1879.

43 For example, British patents: 3484 15/9/1877, 323 23/1/1882, 5464 16/11/1882, 5874 9/12/1882, 1500 22/3/1883, 2059 24/4/1883, 4566 8/3/1884, 7789 16/5/1884.

44 For example, British patents: 777 3/3/1875, 3370 27/9/1875, 3838 4/10/1876, 741 22/2/1877, 1659 28/4/1877, 3763 10/10/1877, 4315 17/11/1877, 807 27/2/1878, 2841 16/7/1878, 2872 18/7/1878.

45 For example, British patents: 1018 24/3/1868, 340 28/1/1873, 2451 7/7/1875, 232 18/1/1877, 3503 12/8/1881, 3896 8/9/1881, 876 23/2/1882, 1419 24/3/1882,

4603 28/9/1882, 1588 29/3/1883, 3304 4/7/1883, 4680 2/10/1883, 5228 3/11/1883, 4241 1/3/1884, 6078 8/4/1884, 739 19/1/1885, 4091 31/3/1885, 5335 30/4/1885, 6418 26/5/1885, 9769 18/8/1885, 32 1/1/1887, 4880 1/4/1887, 17995 31/12/1887, 4250 20/3/1888.

46 Navin, *Whitin Machine Works,* pp. 180–203. British Patent 737, 18/3/1871. USA Patent 113,575,11/4/1871.

47 Leigh, *Modern Cotton Spinning,* p. 235. Note that the figure for mules is with the spindle speed averaged out over the cycle, the actual speed would be higher than 5,000 rpm. The origin of these figures is not stated but they may come from Sawyer.

48 Nasmith, *Modern Cotton Spinning Machinery,* p. 241. Although there are records of Howard & Bullough included in the Platt-Saco-Lowell Archive (LRO DDPSL) none date back this far. No British Patent for the Rabbeth spindle as such can be traced but 807 27/2/1878 to John Bullough of Accrington, communicated by Francis Rabbeth of Pawtucket, Rhode Island, USA, makes modifications to this spindle.

49 LRO DDPSL/1/42/5 p. 247 1/3/1886.

50 Platt Brothers & Co. Ltd, *Catalogue of Cotton Spinning and Weaving Machinery, with Calculations, &c.* (Oldham: Platt Brothers & Co. Ltd, 1929), pp. 323–4. Note that the mule spindle speeds given here will be actual rather than effective speeds, effective speeds would be around 66% of the speeds quoted here.

51 Marsden, *Cotton Spinning,* pp. 312–14. This book was first published in 1884 and reprinted regularly until 1909, and possibly later, without any alteration to the text which became increasingly out of date at each reprint. Although there are records of Brooks & Doxey included in the Platt-Saco-Lowell Archive (LRO DDPSL) none date back this far.

52 English Patent 7388 12/6/1837 John George Bodmer.

53 Holden, *Stott & Sons,* pp. 104–5. Since the publication of this book it has been found that Platt Brothers produced one frame to this design in 1898 for Holdsworth & Gibb of Moorside Mills, Swinton (LRO DDPSL/1/42/10 p. 118 22/10/1898). Strictly speaking this was not a ring frame, but a flexible flyer frame.

54 British Patents 876 23/2/1882 and 2838 16/6/1882 George Perkins, George Wimpenny and Joseph Hampson Evans.

55 LRO DDPSL/1/42/5–11.

56 LRO DDPSL/1/42/7 p. 367.

57 Platt, *Catalogue of Cotton Spinning and Weaving Machinery,* p. 229.

58 Saco-Lowell Shops, *Cotton Machinery* (Boston, MA: Saco-Lowell Shops, 1920), pp. 369–438.

59 Nasmith, *Modern Cotton Spinning Machinery,* pp. 253–5.

60 The Cotton Board, *Modernisation in the Cotton Spinning Industry* (Manchester: The Cotton Board, 1947), p. 32.

61 In interpreting such figures it should be pointed out there was less demand for the finer counts of yarn, the largest demand being for counts under 40.

62 See for example: 'S.E.B', 'The Development of Ring Spinning: Its Present and Future Position', *Textile Manufacturer* 15 (15 December 1889), p. 567–8.

63 The earliest known order is LRO DDPSL/1/42/1, p. 46, September 1864 for Jas. W. & A. Taylor of Barnard Castle, Co. Durham but no earlier order books have survived, so we cannot be certain that this is the first order.

64 LRO DDPSL/1/42/1 (the first order for Harmony Mills, with copy of letter, is p. 127). LRO DDPSL/1/42/2 (see p. 103 for J.B. Wood order. This ignores a machine made Jan. 1877, p. 69, for Platt Brothers for 'experiment').

65 Nasmith, *Modern Cotton Spinning Machinery,* p. 239.
66 DDPSL/2/26/1 p. 208, 24 April 1873. The ultimate destination for this order is not know because it is in the name of John M. Summner & Co., Manchester, who were export agents. Note this order book for throstles starts in 1851 so we can be certain that this is the first ring and traveller frame order.
67 LRO DDPSL/2/26/2 p. 279; DDPSL/1/42/6 p. 389.
68 John Worrall Ltd, *The Cotton Spinners and Manufacturers' Directory for Lancashire* (Oldham: John Worrall Ltd, 27th edn, 1911), pp. 333–353.
69 J. S. Toms, 'Integration, Innovation, and the Progress of a Family Cotton Enterprise: Fielden Brothers Ltd, 1889–1914', *Textile History,* 27 (1996), pp. 77–100. Brian Law, *Fieldens of Todmorden* (Littleborough: George Kelsall, 1995), pp. 111, 135, 286–287.
70 J. S. Toms, 'Growth, Profits and Technological Choice: The Case of the Lancashire Cotton Textile Industry', *Journal of Industrial History,* 1 (1998), pp. 35–55.
71 John Worrall Ltd, *The Cotton Spinners and Manufacturers' Directory for Lancashire* (Oldham: John Worrall Ltd, 27th edn, 1911), p. 241.
72 L. J. Mills, *Practical Ring Spinning* (Manchester: Emmott & Co. Ltd, 1922), p. 357–8.
73 'S.E.B.', 'Development of Ring Spinning'.
74 'The Advance of Ring Spinning', *Textile Manufacturer* (34, 15 November 1908), p. 361.
75 Thornley, *Self-Acting Mules,* p. viii. Thomas Thornley, *Advanced Cotton Spinning* (London: Scott, Greenwood & Son, 1923), pp. 331–332. W. Lawrence Balls, *Studies of Quality in Cotton* (London: Macmillan & Co. Ltd, 1928), p. 91. Allan Ormerod, *An Industrial Odyssey* (Manchester: The Textile Institute, 1996), p. 14. J. Buckley, *Modern Cotton Spinning and Doubling Machinery* (Oldham: Platt Brothers & Co. Ltd, 1944).
76 See, for example, the machines advertised by Rieter (www. rieter. ch).
77 W. Klein, *Manual of Textile Technology Short-staple Spinning Series, vol. 1: The Technology of Shortstaple Spinning* (Manchester: The Textile Institute, n. d. [c. 1990]), pp. 35–6. W. Klein, *Manual of Textile Technology Short-staple Spinning Series, vol. 5: New Spinning Systems* (Manchester: The Textile Institute, 1993), pp. 1, 24, 48. Textile Month, November 2002, p. 18–19.
78 For example: William Lazonick, 'Factor Costs and the Diffusion of Ring Spinning in Britain Prior to World War I', *Quarterly Journal of Economics,* 96 (1981), p. 97, refers in passing to the throstle as 'an antiquated ancestor of ring spindle'.
79 Lars G. Sandberg, 'American Rings and English Mules: The Role of Economic Rationality', *Quarterly Journal of Economics,* 83 (1969), p. 25.
80 Toms, 'Growth, Profits and Technological Choice', pp. 40–41.
81 William Lazonick, 'Industrial Organization and Technological Change: The Decline of the British Cotton Industry', *Business History Review,* 57 (1983), pp. 195–236.
82 Sandberg, 'American Rings and English Mules', pp. 41–42.
83 Roger N. Holden, A *Historical Study of Chadderton Mill* (Unpublished essay: 2001), pp. 16, 22 (copy available at Oldham Local Studies Library).
84 William Lazonick, 'Production Relations, Labor Productivity, and Choice of Technique: British and US Cotton Spinning', *Journal of Economic History,* 41 (1981), pp. 492–516.

85 Glyn Jones, *The Millers* (Lancaster: Carnegie, 2001), pp. 4, 11.

86 Gross, *The Course of Industrial Decline*. Tamara K. Hareven and Randolph Langenbach, *Amoskeag: Life and Work in an American Factory-City* (Hanover, NH: University Press of New England, 2nd edn, 1995).

87 Had William Lazonick taken this salutary exercise before writing his 1981 article 'Production Relations, Labor Productivity, and Choice of Technique', he would have found 10 or 12 mills still operating in Oldham, all ring spinning, but probably less in Fall River.

3 Industrial Relations and Technical Change

Profits, Wages and Costs in the Lancashire Cotton Industry, 1880–1914

Stephen Procter and Steven Toms

Introduction

The institutional perspective sees the UK's economic decline in the twentieth century as rooted in the rigidities established at the end of the nineteenth. According to Elbaum and Lazonick, the competitive capitalism which had served Britain well in the earlier parts of the nineteenth century failed to transform itself into the corporate capitalism necessary for success by the century's end.[1] From an institutional perspective the Lancashire cotton industry provides a classic example of this predicament. Its first basic weakness, argues Lazonick, lay in its industrial organization.[2] The vertical specialization that characterized the industry – in particular, the split between cotton spinners and cotton weavers – meant that there did not exist the co-ordination of decision-making necessary to replace traditional methods of production with the new technologies of ring spinning and automatic looms. This, it is argued, was a situation which persisted well into the twentieth century and which saw the industry unable in the end to withstand the pressures of foreign competition.

This view of the nature and impact of the structure of organizations has more recently been called into question.[3] Higgins and Toms, for example, have provided evidence which suggests that vertical specialization in the industry was associated with superior financial performance.[4] Debate on this issue is likely to continue but it is not our intention here to be part of it. If we accept at least that the institutionalist perspective on the relationship between organization structure and competitive advantage is not beyond question, this places a greater emphasis on a second part of their case: the role of industrial relations in the long-term decline of the UK economy.

For Lazonick, the cotton industry in the last quarter of the nineteenth and the first part of the twentieth century was one in which workers were well-organized and able to impose their demands on employers.[5] In this account, trade unions were able to exploit the system of wage lists around which negotiations in the industry were structured. Employers did derive some benefits from this system – it offered a defence against both damaging price wars and workers' collectively reducing the pace of work – and were to some extent also able to circumvent it by the use of inferior cotton inputs or 'bad spinning'. Nonetheless, just as in the case of industrial organization, the institutionalist argument is that even into the 1960s management was constrained in technological innovation by the system of industrial relations established at the end of the previous century.

This part of the institutional case thus needs to be considered along-side those who see this system of industrial relations as being of central importance in the UK's more general technological backwardness. Prime amongst these are Kilpatrick and Lawson, who argue that the early accept-ance of trade unionism in the UK meant that by the beginning of the twen-tieth century even 'new' unions of unskilled workers had followed the craft-based unions in establishing customs and norms which predated and thus resisted the introduction of mass production techniques.[6] The policy of British management was to conciliate rather than challenge this power, the effect being to damage the economy's capacity for innovation and hence its potential for growth.

These views have not of course gone unchallenged. For one thing, the Kilpatrick and Lawson thesis suffers from a lack of supporting evidence. They make reference to a number of industry case studies but on closer examination these appear to offer them little support.[7] Other authors have attacked the arguments themselves. Coates drew attention to the 'employ-ers' offensive' of the 1890s, and argues also that it is 'almost impossible' for any substantial workplace power possessed by trade unions to have survived in the widespread and persistent unemployment of the 1920s and 1930s.[8] Hyman and Elger argue that Kilpatrick and Lawson's is an 'over-romanticized' view of British working class strength, one which ignores the limited nature of any gains it was able to make.[9] Dintenfass emphasizes how in many cases trade unions collaborated with management in such indus-tries as engineering, cotton and coal.[10]

The objective of the present paper is to add weight to those who take issue with the idea that it was employee strength and recalcitrance in the cotton industry that led to its failure to innovate and, in turn, to its long-term decline. To do this the paper divides into three main parts. The first of these examines the transformation in industrial relations in the half century before 1914. It evolved in this period from an individualistic, sometimes paternalis-tic environment in which utopian inspired co-operative organizational struc-tures briefly flourished, into a highly institutionalized, federated system.

In the second main part of the paper we turn to the balance of power within this system of industrial relations. The evidence presented is drawn from accounting records, a source not commonly exploited in labour history. Such neglect would be surprising in any case, given the usefulness of this type evidence for assessing the outcomes of bargaining processes. It is particular surprising in the case of the cotton industry in this period, for it is precisely around issues of accounting information that the system of industrial relations was structured.

Using similar accounts-based data, the third main part of the paper addresses the question of technological change more directly. The evidence presented here suggests that because employers were doing well out of the existing system they had little incentive to introduce new technologies. A full examination of the labour costs associated with the spinning process – taking into account the necessary attendant processes as well as the spinning itself – shows that the introduction of the new ring-spinning technologies was difficult to justify. In looking for an explanation of the Lancashire industry's technological 'backwardness', we conclude, it is thus at employer policy rather than employee resistance that our attention should be directed.

From Co-operative Organization to Industrial Relations

The co-operative principle upon which many Lancashire business organizations had been founded since the 1840s reinforced the subsequent development of 'working class limiteds'.[11] Their rise and fall had important implications for the evolution of industrial relations in the cotton industry which are analysed in this section.

The experience of the Rochdale 'pioneers' in distributive co-operatives encouraged similar ventures in the field of production. A prominent example, the Rochdale Co-operative Manufacturing Society, later known as the Mitchell Hey mill was established as a co-operative in 1854. All the promoters were members of the Society, and all employees were shareholders and surpluses were paid as a bonus to labour.[12] Similar developments six years later led to the establishment of the Sun Mill Company, formed in 1859. Its founders, the members of the Oldham Industrial Co-operative Society, led by the idealistic William Marcroft, gave the new company a democratic structure designed to foster the principles of producer co-operation and employee control. Management of the company was by means of elected committees, for example along the lines of responsibility for different parts of the balance sheet, namely the 'Fixed Stock' and 'Saleable Stock' committees.[13]

Such democratic principles obviated the need for shopfloor trade union organization and must at least partly explain why Oldham District operatives shunned industry-wide trade unions in the 1850s and 1860s.[14] Union organization remained problematic for several decades due to worker share ownership in the new 'democratic' limiteds. The limited liability principle, to which the co-operators also subscribed following the Companies Acts of 1856 and 1862, was seen as an adjunct of co-operation. Working class investment was thereby reinforced and following the flotation of sixty new mills in the 1873–5 period, the methods of organization, management and accounting were direct imitations of the co-operative societies.[15] Thus in 1873 75% of shares in these mills were owned by working class investors, although this proportion declined towards the end of the decade. A couple of years later total investors in Oldham numbered 10,000, or one in five of the population.[16]

Contradictions in co-operative principles meant that the prominent experiments were shortlived. Thus few workers owned shares in their own companies for long. When Gladstone visited Sun Mill in 1867 only 4 out of 1,000 shareholders were also employees and he observed '. . . this company is not really a co-operative one, but an association of small capitalists'.[17] At Mitchell Hey, the co-operative principles also began to decline in the 1860s. As is common with many co-operative organizations, scale and industrial democracy acted in contradiction.[18] A new group of working class shareholders created through a share issue for a second mill, objected to the payment of dividends to labour. As many worked at other mills, where they had no similar right to these bonuses, they were keen to end the practice. In 1862, after two previous unsuccessful votes, a majority succeeded in abolishing the labour bonus principle.[19] Nonetheless, cotton operatives continued to be significant contributors to the share lists of other companies floated under the limited liability acts[20] and these early associations had an important influence on the development of industrial relations in Lancashire.

The 1870s was a transitional decade in this respect, with two conflicting forces at work; the traditional institutional structures of co-operation and the adoption of wage lists. Democratic governance structures were adopted which meant that characteristically, there was wide public participation at company meetings, in new issues, and in the buying and selling of existing shares.[21] Democratic structure was maintained via a 'one member one vote' system at quarterly shareholders' meetings. Directors' salaries were kept to a small fraction of those earned in other industries in companies owned by, as Potter put it, 'upper class' shareholders.[22] Democratic norms were further underpinned by mechanisms such as limits on maximum shareholdings, proxy holdings, and anonymous institutional or nominee investors.[23] At the same time, the expertise and technical knowledge became increasingly important for both worker/shareholders and operatives. For the former, participatory governance mechanisms provided the opportunity to apply shopfloor based scrutiny, thought by some to contribute towards improved efficiency.[24] For the latter, the emergence of the list system meant increasing reliance on union officials who were skilled technicians. Like 'the valuer or accountant' such experts took a highly professional view of their duties.[25]

For the overwhelming majority of Oldham operatives, it was reliance on union officials rather than participation in company management that became the *modus operandi*. The trade cycle, its associated uncertainties and the redistributions of wealth, was the driving force. The depression of 1877–9 discouraged working class equity investment as share values fell, although the companies themselves survived.[26] As union membership increased working class equity investment declined, the worker-shareholders were treated with suspicion on the shop floor.[27] Meanwhile, booms tended to be associated with the promotion of more secretive, narrowly controlled companies.[28] Working class disillusionment with share ownership became complete in the 1890s which saw an 'unparalleled depression and of severity and duration'.[29] Between late 1890 and early 1895 an index of the Oldham stock market fell almost continuously for forty eight months, before finally reaching a pre war low in March 1896.[30] Poorer investors were unable to meet calls from the cash strapped limited companies and former share owning operatives turned increasingly to the security offered by trade union organization.

The Balance of Power in Industrial Relations: Evidence from Outcomes

The Brooklands Agreement

The period 1870 to 1890 had witnessed several important trends. These were a shift from North East to South East Lancashire as the main focus of developing trade union organization,[31] the adoption of wage lists, the decline of employer paternalism and the linked rise of employer federations, and the rise of federal bargaining structures. Increasingly tempestuous industrial relations culminated in the 'Brooklands Lockout', the subsequent agreement in 1893 and the institutionalization of bargaining thereafter. An important feature of the new system was its promotion of employer and operative collaboration to further collective interests, for example through political lobbying.[32] The pattern of dispute and the agreements that ended them, were predicated on the vulnerability of the industry to the business cycle.[33] Therefore the Employers' Federation had a strong incentive to suggest that profits were lower than they really were.[34] Meanwhile the operatives, and especially the spinners, were wedded to an economic doctrine that suggested these profits fixed the maximum possible wage.[35] Such a combination of attitudes suggests, given the asymmetry of accounting information, the employers were in a better position to exploit the new bargaining structures and that despite their creation of a closed union labour aristocracy, the operative spinners representatives were in a poor position to protect the wages of their members. In this section we explore this possibility through an analysis of winners and losers following the agreement.

In response to Brooklands, employers increasingly centralized the indoor management of their companies. As the problems of agreeing as to the 'state of trade' persisted into the 1900s,[36] directors' coups eliminated the last vestiges of democratic ownership in the Oldham companies. From now on it was necessary to operate with greater secrecy towards the workforce.[37] With centralization of capital ownership came growth in employers' associations. Previously democratically controlled companies became the driving force, first with the establishment of the centralized United Cotton Spinners Association and later the Federation of Master Cotton Spinners Associations.[38]

As the demands of workers and employers became increasingly channelled into formalized bargaining structures, it is interesting to speculate as to which side tended to benefit the more. The evidence suggests that despite increasing solidarity expressed through shop floor organization, the employers benefited more from the Brooklands compromise. As the agreement institutionalized piece rates, wages remained linked to the efficiency of the industry and were also variable depending on the stage of the trade cycle.

Trends in Real Wages

These reasons partly explain why at a time when cotton profits were better than in the rest of the economy, particularly in the period 1896–1914, Lancashire cotton operatives achieved smaller increases in real wages than did workers in other sectors.[39] Table 3.1 shows that as profits for British industry as a whole declined, the cotton sector experienced a rising trend. Unlike other sectors by and large, especially in its dramatic climax of 1907, returns were quite spectacular[40] and must have had a profound influence on the cotton investor. Whereas cotton investors were rewarded by far better returns after 1896, the picture for employees was more ambivalent. As for the rest of the economy, the upward trend in real wages, defined in terms of the difference between money wages and the cost of living, which had begun with the industrial revolution, came to an apparent end after 1900 (Table 3.2 and Figure 3.1).

Table 3.1 Rates of return to capital, British cotton and manufacturing industry

	% Five year average return to capital	
	British industry	*Cotton*
1885–89	14.50	5.74
1890–94	11.30	5.70
1895–99	10.80	7.56
1900–1904	7.10	6.13
1905–9	7.20	11.72
1910–13	7.90	8.63
Whole period	9.87	7.61
Std dev	2.68	3.96

Sources: Cotton industry, Toms, thesis, p. 28; British industry averages, Davis, L. and Huttenback, R., *Mammon and the Pursuit of Empire: The Economics of British Imperialism* (Cambridge, 1988), p. 117.

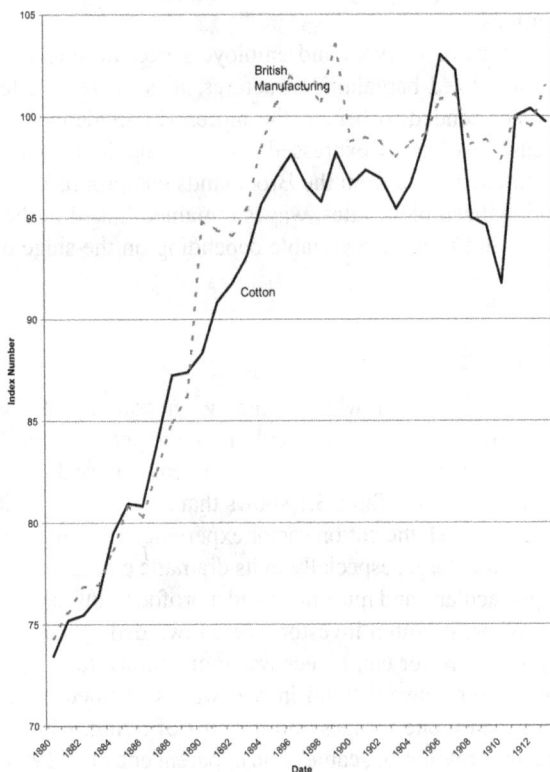

Figure 3.1 Real Wages, 1880–1913

Sources: As for Table 3.2

Table 3.2 Real wages, 1880–1913

	Percentage annual growth rate		
	Cotton Industry	Manufacturing Industry	British Industry
1882–1899	1.48	1.67	1.71
1900–1913	0.23	0.19	0.58

Sources: Cotton and manufacturing, calculated from Feinstein, 'New estimates of earnings', table 4, pp. 608–11 and 'A new look at the cost of living', table 4, pp. 170–1; UK economy, Feinstein, 'What really happened to real wages', table 4, p. 344.

The trend in Figure 3.1 has important implications for our understanding of the evolution of industrial relations. Especially in the spinning section, cotton trade unions have been considered a good example of a craft based labour aristocracy.[41] However, the evidence in Table 3.2 and Figure 3.1 suggests that cotton workers were poorly rewarded relative to the manufacturing sector as a whole and the economy in general. Manufacturing was affected as much by the spread of general unionism as it was by the retention of craft control,[42] whereas the general economy included a growing class of professional and salaried workers hitherto unrecognized in the construction of real wages indices.[43] Although the breaks in trend occurred for both cotton and manufacturing around 1900, cotton had been lagging behind for about a decade. We have commented elsewhere that cotton suffered badly in the depression of the early 1890s, and it is evident from Figure 3.1 that contemporaries were incorrect to blame the trade unions for the plight of the industry and the crash in share values,[44] as relative wages were falling, albeit perhaps not as steeply as the employers would have liked.

If the Brooklands agreement had stabilized industrial relations,[45] it did so at the expense of the stability of wages themselves. By implicitly linking wage advances and reductions to the trade cycle, but at the same time limiting them to one per year and to a maximum of five per cent,[46] the agreement helped ensure that wages fluctuated, but with nothing like the variation in profits. Thus cotton wages raced ahead in the boom of 1904–7 relative to other groups, but then fell dramatically again in the slump of 1909–10. However, in relation to generally improving profits, the share of extra wealth accruing to labour was low, and adjusted only slowly so that the benefit of the 5% advance of June 1907 was shortlived and by July 1908 the employers were already pushing for a reduction.[47] Support for trade federations and collective action on wages must have contributed towards higher profits for the rising class of cotton financial capitalists, and probably outweighed the benefits of previously paternalistic management style.[48] In so far that this was a deliberate and forced response to an apparent increase in the bargaining power of the operatives,[49] the Brooklands agreement would appear to have been an effective management response for the maintenance of profitability. The 'company town' and paternalistic management styles were declining in this period,[50] and the attractiveness of the new bargaining system and its associated employer solidarity may have accentuated the process.

For cotton workers, craft unionism and its industry wide accommodation with employers' federations at Brooklands, thus appeared to offer little benefit. The Leninist argument of 'embourgoisification',[51] the rising wealth of the working class creating a mood for the acceptance of reformist ideas, did not apply in the strict sense. Election of reformist trade union officials before 1890, according to one view, was the result of narrowing margins after 1873 and the need felt by employers for an industrial *detente*.[52] Mutual interest policies culminated in the compromise at Brooklands when Macara and Mawdsley, representing the two sides, struck up a lasting friendship, and an agreement which, 'pointed the way . . . to that industrial harmony which arises from wise statesmanship and eschews the weapon of force'.[53]

However, the union leaders' policies of employer collaboration subsequently created conditions which led a relative fall in real wages for cotton operatives in the 1900s at a time of rising profits for the employers. Even so, as the conditions which had led to the rise of collaboration went into reverse, there was no return to increased militancy. From 1893 the characteristic mood was of 'industrial peace';[54] even the boom of 1907 failed to produce strikes associated with wage demands, and signs of growing disaffection were only apparent in the very last years before the 1914–18 war.[55] Overall it is difficult to conclude that the system of industrial relations acted as a barrier to cost cutting employer strategies.[56] The Brooklands system provided the employers with a satisfactory mechanism for keeping wages under control.

The Shift to Profits

Although generalization about trends is difficult where the trade cycle played such an important role, the real wages trend is suggestive of a shift to profits at the expense of wages. A rising trend of return to capital and of cotton share prices[57] in conjunction with Figure 3.1 suggested that capital gained at labour's expense in the 1900s. Evidence from the accounting records of cotton companies provides tentative support for this hypothesis (Table 3.3). Using profit and loss account data, the proportions of net value added[58] shared by capital (measured by profit, interest and depreciation) and labour (wages and salaries) were calculated and compared for two dates, 1898 and 1912.[59] Between these dates the real wage trend was relatively flat

Table 3.3 Capital, labour and value added, 1898–1912

	Spinning		Weaving	
	1898	*1912*	*1898*	*1912*
(1) Percentage shares of value added				
Wages	55.7	54.4	79.7	75.4
Capital	44.3	45.6	20.3	24.6
	100.0	100.0	100.0	100.0
(2) Percentages to sales				
Wages	15.1	10.8	23.2	15.4
Material	65.1	73.1	62.3	75.1
Capital	11.8	8.8	5.9	5.1
Other Expenses	8.0	7.3	8.6	4.4
	100.0	100.0	100.0	100.0

Sources: Calculated from company accounts, sources per table 1.2. (1) For each company and for each year, material and non wage expenses (excluding profits, interest, and depreciation) were subtracted from sales to obtain value added. Wages calculated as percentage of value added with capital share treated as the residual. (2) Each profit and loss expense item calculated as a percentage of sales. Capital defined as the total of profits, interest and depreciation.

(Figure 3.1). Averaging calculations for the six years before 1898 and 1912 suggested that the figures were representative. The results of these calculations are shown in Table 3.3.

Data presented in Table 3.3 confirm the hypothesis of a shift to capital. However, the shift was very slight, and since evidence was available for only five companies in total, it would be wrong to attempt to read too much into the figures. The safest interpretation might be that there was at least a stability in the respective shares of value added but more likely a shift to capital. At a national level the shift to capital hypothesis has been supported by considering the rising trend in interest rates in conjunction with the flat trend in real wages.[60] Use of new data has called this interpretation into question, and it has been argued that nominal GDP per worker was rising in the Edwardian period.[61] However, the likelihood of sectoral variation was also suggested, in particular cotton, which might have experienced a shift to profits on the basis of its export boom.[62] Accordingly investors and entrepreneurs experienced substantial rewards in this period via rising share prices in Lancashire and increased returns to capital, in contrast to the relatively slower increase in real wages.

Productivity Trends

Workers did even worse relatively if increases in productivity, which the list system supposedly ensured were shared between the two sides of industry,

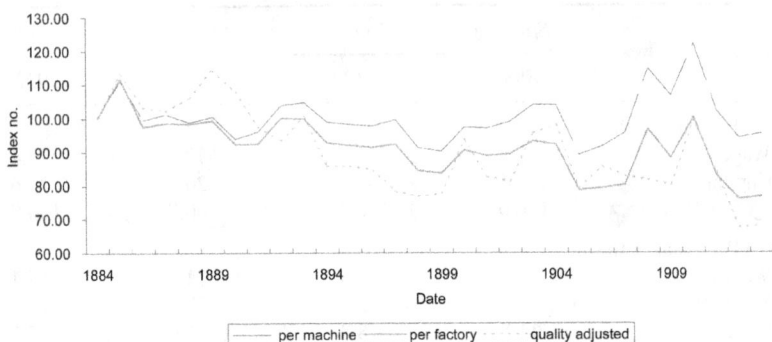

Figure 3.2 Capital Output Ratios, 1884–1913

Sources: Based on yarn produced and consumed, machines on an index of spindles and looms (1 loom weighted at 60 spindles) and no. of firms per Jones, Increasing Return, p. 277; output adjusted for quality per Sandberg, 'Movements in quality', pp. 10–11.

are also taken into account. Figure 3.2 charts an improvement in efficiency as a function of quality improvements and the development of larger factories. It also shows that where output was measured purely on a per spindle basis there was no clear trend for capital output ratio and therefore no apparent improvement in productivity.[63] However, this is too simplistic, as it ignores both factory layout and economies of scale associated with putting more mules or looms into larger factories, as well as any effective slowing down of machines associated with increased quality.[64] Where output was calculated in relation to the number of factories, the resulting capital output ratio declined steeply (Figure 3.2). Furthermore, if output quality is taken into account, there was a further decline in the capital output ratio. Overall, the line which tends to slope downwards most prominently from left to right in Figure 3.2 is that which shows the combined effects of quality and larger factories.

All three measures in Figure 3.2 show downward slopes and cyclical effects of varying degrees. Factors such as machine speed ups, mule lengthening, factory layout, and quality shifts created the opportunities for marginal improvements in capital productivity. For labour productivity, the cyclical character of the industry makes measurement more problematic. During upswings the industry apparently became much more efficient as full capacity was approached.[65] Corresponding declines occurred in the troughs of recessions, but over a longer period the increase in productivity is still apparent.[66] On the output per operative basis steep increases in productivity occurred during the upswing of the trade cycle, as acknowledged by Sandberg.[67] The use of labour productivity evidence from this period to prove stagnation in the industry is thus questionable. What appears clearer is that the institutionalized wage bargaining system protected employers from wage advances in periods of higher capacity and rising productivity.

The shift from labour to capital suggested above appears more convincing when considered in relation to productivity data. This is confirmed further by the statistics in Table 3.4. In spinning, capital was very rapidly attracted in the 1900s in response, no doubt to increasing levels of profitability and output. Also this was influenced by regulated wages and a labour cost function that was slow to rise in periods of prosperity. Labour input meanwhile grew only slowly in the period 1890–1914 and declined somewhat in the 1890s. In weaving there was also a loss of labour input during the years of depression. However, when the recovery came, it was this section of the industry, with its predominantly female labour force,[68] which saw a major expansion in numbers employed. In the unprecedented export booms of 1905–7 and 1911–13, there was an over commitment of capital in the case of spinning, and labour in the case of weaving.

Table 3.4 Cotton industry; total factor productivity, 1884–1913

(1) TFP analysis – spinning			
	Output	*Labour*	*Capital*	*Residual*
1884–1899	1.18	0.52	0.47	0.19
1900–1913	1.56	0.52	0.46	0.58
Overall	1.58	0.48	0.49	0.61
(2) TFP analysis – weaving			
	Output	*Labour*	*Capital*	*Residual*
1884–1899	1.34	0.62	0.30	0.42
1900–1913	1.39	0.61	0.30	0.48
Overall	1.67	0.57	0.28	0.62
(3) Annual compounded growth rates (%)			
Spinning			
	Output	*Labour*	*Capital*	
1884–1899	1.04	–0.39	0.25	
1900–1913	3.23	1.07	2.27	
Overall	1.54	0.29	1.22	
Weaving			
	Output	*Labour*	*Capital*	
1884–1899	1.85	–1.16	1.15	
1900–1913	2.38	3.04	1.37	
Overall	1.74	0.77	1.29	

Sources: Output, spinning yarn production per Jones, *Increasing return*, table II, p. 275, weaving, cotton piece goods exports per Robson, *The cotton industry in Britain*, table A1, p. 331. and as adjusted by the yarn and cloth quality indices respectively, per Sandberg, 'Movements in the quality', tables 2 and 4, pp. 10–11; capital based on index of total capital employed, sources as per Figure 3.2; capital and labour weights in (1) per table 10.5; labour data as per table 10.7.

Industrial Relations and Technical Change

Our analysis so far suggests that it is unlikely that it was trade union strength that accounted for British firms' reluctance to adopt the new production technologies. Having also cast doubt on the idea that vertical specialization in the industry was the key factor, we turn now to a more direct consideration of firms' decisions in this area. According to the Lazonick hypothesis, saving on raw material input was an important reason for adherence to the mule. Trade union inflexibility and the minder-piecer system prevented the reorganization of work to achieve labour cost savings; at the same time the system was threatened by the availability of ring spinning. Masters and men therefore co-operated to achieve the best productivity possible through raw material savings, for example in the agreement for bad spinning compensation in the Brooklands agreement of 1893.[69]

Whilst providing a plausible theory, this argument is not backed by evidence from Rochdale, the early centre of British ring spinning. It is noteworthy first of all that those making the experimental moves in ring spinning did not cite labour cost as a source of saving. Rather, the Rochdale entrepreneurs justified their investment in rings in terms of savings in raw material input without any loss of quality, low breakdown and maintenance cost, and the relative cheapness of the machinery.[70] In Rochdale, and elsewhere, raw material saving was given as a key reason for the introduction of the ring. Had Lancashire entrepreneurs wished to compete against the threat of low wage competition from overseas on the basis of savings in raw material input, the ring spindle would have given them the means of doing so for the lower range of counts.

On the other hand, using the ring spindle did not provide the early ring spinning companies with an easy way round the increased institutionalization of industrial relations. Their entrepreneurs relied on paternalism rather than exploitation, but at the same time sought solidarity with employers elsewhere in the industry. Such contradictions were keenly felt throughout Lancashire, especially where joint stock companies were prevalent.[71] As elsewhere, Milnrow, the location of the earliest ring spinning companies, had many of the characteristics of a 'company town'. Like the Ashtons of Hyde and the Fieldens of Todmorden, the Heaps of Milnrow exercised a good deal of local deferential and political influence, as manifested in the local reaction to the death of the founding entrepreneur.[72] Yet only a few days earlier the hands employed at his New Ladyhouse, the New Hey and the Haugh spinning mills had been placed on a week's notice. Local management acted at the behest of the Masters' Federation, which had decided to stop the mills until the settlement of the Stalybridge dispute. In addition to the Milnrow ring spinners, mule spinning mills such as the nearby Garfield were also involved.[73] Whatever reason Heap and Tweedale had for promoting the ring spindle at Milnrow, it was not because they sought to drive down wages, nor was it to escape from the increasingly institutionalized structure of labour relations.

In order to gain further insight, and to reassess the apparent contradictions arising from the above discussion in further detail, it is useful to compare actual cost structures of ring and mule companies. Ring and mule labour cost statistics for the late 1880s and early 1890s, based on the Milrow companies and other mule and ring mills in nearby Oldham, show that the labour content of their output was actually *higher* in the 1880s and 1890s than for mule spindles.[74] Unlike the paternalist managements of the Milnrow mills, potential emulators may not have had a generous attitude towards expensive, and perhaps locally scarce, ring spinning labour. Comparative data, in terms of spindles per hand also suggests the early ring spinners had a greater labour intensity than mule spindle concerns. The higher productivity of ring spindles meant that labour formed an approximately equal proportion of total cost. Expensive labour in the context of ring spinning directly contradicts the usual understanding of the development of this technology.

Labour cost savings, given the faster speed of the ring spindle, may have been available in the spinning process itself. However, ring spinning required more labour in roving and other preparation stages and in subsequent processes, such as doffing and winding.[75] Where ring spinning developed from throstle spinning, as in Rochdale and other areas, there was a tradition of labour intensity, particularly with regard to doffing.[76] Doffing was an unskilled task and was usually carried out by teams (four per machine) of young and inexperienced workers.[77] It was their employment that to the apparent labour intensity of ring spinning. Evidence from the Rochdale district can be corroborated by international comparisons. A ring spinning mill in France in 1882 producing 30s twist had a spindle per operative ratio of 75,[78] and was thus directly comparable in labour intensity with the New Ladyhouse spinning company at 79, but well below the level of 206 achieved by the typical Oldham mule spinner.

That labour cost saving was not a strategy associated with the introduction of ring spinning was confirmed by contrasts of costs between the ring mills themselves. The New Ladyhouse mill was the most profitable of the three Milnrow concerns, yet it was also the most labour intensive.[79] Profits may have been improved by the relatively low average wage, which in turn may have reflected the application of piece rates to at least some of the hands. Even so, workers were paid more here on average than in the strongholds of labour aristocracy in the mule mills of Oldham. James Heap would have been regarded as a generous employer and the public grief apparently expressed by the whole town on his death may have run deeper, and for reasons beyond those of pure paternalism, than guessed at by the newspaper correspondent.[80] Expensive labour cost may have been compounded by the absence of a comprehensive, institutionalized wage list coupled with the relative scarcity of ring spinners. Highly individual lists for ring spinners existed by the early 1900s. Following industrial action, the final moves towards a universal official list for ring spinners' wages were not made until 1912.[81] Moreover, the same factor may have led to variation in wages over time and by geographical area. Thus, although wage structures were important, as far as the early experiments in ring spinning were concerned, they were not decisive. The new ring mills might well have employed female labour and probably young girls to doff the machines; they were hardly sweatshops though, and labour cost savings were patently not the reason for the introduction of ring spinning.

Relative expense of ring mill labour may also have been a product of cheap labour in the mule spinning section of the industry. As an oft quoted example of a labour aristocrat,[82] relatively high wages in the mule room were confined to the senior minder. Out of his own wage, he would effectively sub-contract his two assistants, the big piecer and little piecer, both of whom depended on promotion up this hierarchy.[83] Both earned relatively low wages,[84] and would have depressed the average wage per hand. Thus

Table 3.5 Gross margins, ring and mule mills, 1892

| | COMPANY | | |
| | RING | MULE | |
	Haugh £	Hathershaw £	Oldham Twist £
Sales	17,572	23,798	38,092
Cotton cost and charges	12,221	17,491	28,573
	%	%	%
Margin	69.49	73.50	75.0

| | RING | MULE | |
	Fielden £	Werneth £	Osborne £
Sales	13,209	28,378	7,981
Cotton cost and charges	9,094	20,981	5,350
	%	%	%
Margin	68.85	73.93	67.03

Note:(1) For Fielden, in the absence of 1892 data, 1895 was used.
(2) Werneth prepared its trading account on a receipts and payments basis and its purchases fluctuated dramatically, therefore a quarterly average was used based on the previous eight quarterly results.
(3) In all cases raw material costs were adjusted for changes in stock levels.
Sources: Haugh, Hathershaw, and Oldham Twist, calculated from *Oldham Chronicle*, 'Commercial Notes' 2nd January, 1892; Fielden, RMA, 1895; Werneth, OLSL, Misc/42/17, Quarterly reports to members; Osborne, LCRO, DDX/869/3/1, trade, capital and profit and loss accounts.

expensive and cheap labour existed side by side. Whereas the subcontracted payment system might create the risk of double counting when using industry data, and although there was no evidence of this,[85] firm specific published accounting reports could be relied upon to contain only the net labour cost to the firm.

As noted above, saving of raw material input using ring spindles was thought to be important by entrepreneurs. Rings were acknowledged to be more productive on the lower count range.[86] That argument was well supported by evidence from accounting records, with raw material accounting for a significantly lower proportion of production cost in ring mills.[87] Table 3.5 provides a collation of data showing sales, cotton costs, and profit margins for ring and mule mills. When compared with mule mills spinning low counts, such as Hathershaw and Oldham Twist, ring mills tended to show a 4–7% superiority in margin.[88] The comparison was flawed however, as even lower count mule mills were producing higher counts than the ring mills, and also weft yarns. Taking into consideration count differentials, the advantage for ring mill margins would have been greater. Only when compared with Osborne, a fine spinner by Oldham standards and therefore operating on above average margins, did the advantage disappear.[89] High labour cost, averaging just under 15% of total cost, cancelled out the benefit for this company on raw material value added. At the coarse end of the market, margins were much narrower, and hence the ring spinners benefited from higher productivity per unit of cotton input, without having to increase their prices. Bearing the above interpretative difficulties in mind, the superiority of the ring on raw material usage clearly made a net contribution to company profits.

Another factor influencing cost structure was lack of industry concentration, and the very small market share of each firm. Under such circumstances high levels of fixed cost create disproportionately large losses as output falls in a recession. Increasing the scale of operations would accentuate such risks. There was thus a strong incentive to avoid ring spinning where, despite some tentative evidence for the use of piece rates at Milnrow, time based wage rates predominated. By contrast mule spinning was attractive, since labour was paid according to piece rates and the Brooklands agreement specifically allowed wage rates to vary with the trade cycle.[90] Fixed cost was also avoided through vertical specialization, allowing management and administrative costs to remain minimal, the market acting as the co-ordinating mechanism.[91] Lazonick has argued that investment in rings was more likely to occur in integrated firms developing high throughput production.[92] However, under the highly variable demand conditions imposed by the trade cycle, the last thing entrepreneurs needed was the high fixed cost structure that such investment implied.

Previous discussions of the relative merits of ring spinning which have used labour cost in their analysis have thus concentrated too narrowly on the spinning process itself. Under British conditions, if wage cost was a barrier to competitiveness, labour intensity in preparatory and after spinning processes must have been an important reason for the coexistence of the ring and mule for a further generation. In its early years at least, ring spinning was not a route for substitution of labour by capital.

Conclusions

The evidence presented in this paper allows us to consider afresh the issues raised in the introduction. Our first conclusion concerns the state of industrial relations and its impact on the diffusion of new technologies. Union inability to defend real wages and seek major advances in buoyant trading conditions, and where there were increases in labour productivity, may mean that trade unions were weaker than hitherto recognized, that the Brooklands agreement was generally favourable to the employers, and that unions would not have been able to mount any serious challenge to a determined employers' bid to replace mules and power looms with alternative technologies. For industrial relations, this was the opposite to what happened in the period 1867 to 1885, when there was a shift from capital to labour.[93] According to one view, this put pressure on employers and forced them into industry wide bargaining at Brooklands.[94] It would be difficult to blame unions for failure to make investments in alternative technology since their power to resist was low.

Our second conclusion reinforces the first. Looking at the costs associated with the different technologies, the evidence shows that as ring spinning was actually more labour intensive than mule spinning, it could not have had any great appeal to employers seeking to displace labour or circumvent the increasing institutionalization of wage negotiations. Commercially, the superior profits enjoyed by the Milnrow companies resulted from savings on raw material inputs, an advantage that would have been shared by other ring spinning companies. If we are trying to explain why the Lancashire cotton industry appeared slow to adopt the new technologies available to it, it is on the decisions of employers rather than the recalcitrance of employees that our attention should focus.

Notes

1 B. Elbaum and W. Lazonick, 'The Decline of the British Economy: An Institutional Perspective', *Journal of Economic History*, Vol. XLIV, No. 2, 1984, pp. 567–83; B. Elbaum and W. Lazonick, 'An Institutional Perspective on British Decline', in B. Elbaum and W. Lazonick (eds), *The Decline of the British Economy* (Oxford: Oxford University Press: 1986).

2 W. Lazonick, 'The Cotton Industry', in Elbaum and Lazonick, *Decline of the British Economy*, pp. 18–50.

3 G. Saxonhouse and G. Wright, 'New Evidence on the Stubborn English Mule and the Cotton Industry, 1878–1920', *Economic History Review*, Vol. 37, pp. 507–19; G. Saxonhouse and G. Wright, 'Stubborn Mules and Vertical Integration: the Disappearing Constraint?', *Economic History Review*, Vol. 40, pp. 87–93.

4 D. Higgins and S. Toms, 'Firm Structure and Financial Performance: the Lancashire Textile Industry, *c.* 1884–*c.* 1960', *Accounting, Business and Financial History*, Vol. 7, No. 2, pp. 195–232.

5 Lazonick, 'Cotton Industry', pp. 24–27.

6 A. Kilpatrick and T. Lawson, 'On the Nature of Industrial Decline in the UK', *Cambridge Journal of Economics*, Vol. 4, pp. 85–102.

7 In this category we can include the following: M. Berg (ed.), *Technology and Toil in Nineteenth Century Britain* (CSE Books: 1979); R. McKersie and L. Hunter, *Pay, Productivity and Collective Bargaining* (Macmillan: 1973); J. McLean and H. Rush, 'The Impact of Microelectronics on the UK: a Suggested Classification and Illustrative Case Studies', Occasional Paper Series 7, Science Policy Research Unit, University of Sussex.

8 D. Coates, *The Question of UK Decline* (Harvester Wheatsheaf: 1994).

9 R. Hyman and T. Elger, 'Job Controls, the Employers' Offensive and Alternative Strategies', *Capital and Class*, Vol. 15, pp. 115–49.

10 M. Dintenfass, *The Decline of Industrial Britain 1870–1980* (Routledge: 1992).

11 T. Ellison, *The Cotton Trade of Great Britain* (London: Frank Cass: 1886; Reprinted: 1968), p. 134; B. Potter, *The Co-operative Movement in Great Britain* (Aldershot: Gower, 1891; Reprinted, 1987), pp. 126–133.

12 *Rochdale Observer*, 10 May 1890.

13 R. E. Tyson, 'William Marcroft', in D. Jeremy (ed.), *Dictionary of Business Biography* (London: Butterworths: 1984–6), p. 121; R. E. Tyson, 'Sun Mill-a Study in Democratic Investment' (unpublished M.A. Thesis, University of Manchester: 1962), p. 230.

14 The Amalgamated Association of Cotton Spinners, formed in 1853; Webb, *The History of Trade Unionism*, p. 307.

15 D. A. Farnie, *The English Cotton Industry and the World Market* (Oxford: 1979), p. 247–9; Tyson, 'William Marcroft', p. 121.

16 Farnie, *English Cotton*, p. 250.

17 Tyson, 'William Marcroft', p. 121. In 1886 several witnesses to the parliamentary Royal Commission pointed out that there were very few operatives who owned shares, particularly in their own companies (*Royal Commission on the Depression of Trade and Industry*, Reports and Minutes of Evidence (1886), for example, q. 5131).

18 M. Aoki, *The Co-operative Game Theory of the Firm* (Oxford, Clarendon Press: 1984), pp. 54–5.

19 *Rochdale Observer*, 10 May 1890.

20 S. Chapman, *The Lancashire Cotton Industry* (Manchester, Manchester University Press: 1904), p. 231. Those seeking the reconciliation of capital and labour via the worker/shareholder mechanism in the 1850s from various political perspectives were prominent in calling for the introduction of limited liability, J. B. Jefferys, Trends in Business Organisation in Great Britain since 1856, with Special Reference to the Financial Structure of Companies, the Mechanism of Investment and the Relations between the Shareholder and the Company

(unpublished Ph.D. thesis, London University: 1938), p. 33; Select Committee, 1850, q. 837, although admitting that workers potentially had a problem with control over each other and their managements (*ibid*, q. 840).

21 Active participation at meetings was always an important feature of the co-operative movement; J. Foster, *Class Struggle and the Industrial Revolution* (London, Methuen: 1974), p. 222.

22 J. S. Toms, The Finance and Growth of the Lancashire Textile Industry, 1870–1914 (unpublished Ph.D. thesis, University of Nottingham: 1996). In 1912, ratios of directors emoluments to sales for a sample of privately controlled cotton companies ranged from 7.15 per cent at Fielden Brothers (Todmorden) to 1.98 per cent at T and R Eccles (Blackburn) and 1.22 per cent at Horrockses (Preston), West Yorkshire Record Office (WYRO), C353/475, Detailed Accounts, 1890–1914, Lancashire County Record Office (LCRO), 868/7/1, Profit and Loss Accounts and Balance Sheets, 1897–1931, LCRO, DDHs/53, Balance Sheets, 1890–1919; in Oldham, Werneth at 0.34 per cent (calculated as above) was more typical, see B. Potter, *The Co-operative Movement in Great Britain* (Aldershot: 1891; Reprinted: 1987).

23 R. Smith, 'An Oldham Limited Liability Company, 1875–1896', *Business History*, December, Vol. 4 (2) (1961), p. 41.

24 Ellison, *The Cotton Trade*, p. 138. Other companies that were run as 'investment unions' and owned by those who 'know nothing of the business carried on' performed poorly in contrast; *Royal Commission*, 1886, q. 5275.

25 Webb, *The History of Trade Unionism*, pp. 478–9.

26 P. Cottrell, *Industrial Finance 1830–1914: The Finance and Organisation of English Manufacturing Industry* (London, Methuen: 1980), p. 110; Farnie, *English Cotton*, p. 266.

27 J. White, 'Lancashire Cotton Textiles', in C. Wrigley (ed.), *A History of British Industrial Relations* (Brighton, Harvester Press: 1982), p. 216; *Royal Commission on Labour, Minutes of Evidence*, 1892, qq. 95–6, 190–3, 2548, 3608–9.

28 Farnie, *English Cotton*, p. 267.

29 *Textile Mercury*, 21 January 1893, p. 43.

30 A simple average index of 20 Oldham companies, selected from the *Oldham Chronicle* share listing and with a value of 100 at June 1890 had fallen to 50.2 by March 1896. An index for companies quoted on the London stock exchange calculated from the data in K. Smith and G. Horne, 'An index number of securities, 1867–1914', *London and Cambridge Economic Service*, Special Memorandum, No. 37: 1934, columns 1–10, pp. 14–15, showed corresponding figures of 100 and 128.3. This rate of decline in Lancashire was equivalent to the loss of value on the London share market in the crash of 1929–33.

31 H. A. Turner, *Trade Union Growth, Structure and Policy: A Comparative Study of the Cotton Unions* (London, Allen and Unwin: 1962), p. 124.

32 For example, a joint committee was established to consider 'the opening of new markets abroad, the alteration of restrictive tariffs, and other similar matters which may benefit of injure the cotton trade . . .', Brooklands Agreement, 1893, *Board of Trade Report on Wages and Hours of Labour, Part II, Standard Piece Rates*, C. 7567, Vol. XXXI, pp. 9–11.

33 Employers were allowed to move for up to a five per cent reduction in wages; conversely up to a five per cent increase could be requested by employees, as determined by the economic cycle; K. Burgess, *The Origins of British Industrial Relations* (London, Croom Helm: 1975), p. 233.

34 For example in the wages dispute of 1897, the Employers cited heavy losses in justification of a proposed reduction in wages; *Times*, 6 November, 13(v). In response, the operatives' representative argued: 'It may suit the word spinners of the Employers' Committee to air their eloquence in chattering about past losses, but if they are half as practical as they flatter themselves they are, they will drop their wailings and devote their energies to increasing their present gains'; *Times*, 13 November 1897, p. 13 (v).

35 Turner, *Trade Union Growth*, p. 149.

36 H.A. Clegg, *The System of Industrial Relations in Great Britain* (Oxford, Basil Blackwell: 1972), pp. 459–60.

37 For example the directors' coup at Sun Mill in 1905, Tyson, Sun Mill, pp. 295–6. Publication of detailed analysis of accounts, died out during the 1890s. The *Oldham Chronicle*, 31 December 1892, for virtually the last time, analysed the balance sheets of several companies showing profits, payments for cotton and charges, wages, receipts for yarn and waste, depreciation and amounts previously written off machinery, trade debtors and creditors, machinery and buildings valuations, and shareholders and loan holders claims. Apart from isolated instances (for example, the Leesbrook Spinning Company, 29 December 1894, 30 March 1895) the practice effectively ceased from 1893 onwards.

38 Turner, *Trade Union Growth*, pp. 146 and 374. The card room strikes at Sun, Hey and Neville mills in 1889 spread to 143 mills with the backing of organised short time; Tyson, Sun Mill, p. 267. The increasing collusion of the employers was also a response to the frequent cornering of the raw cotton market by Liverpool merchants, *ibid*, p. 271.

39 Some have suggested that the structural break in the British economy of the 1890s was associated with a change in trend of real wages. The levelling of previously rising living standards was associated with the stagnation of British industry, W. Lewis, *Economic Survey, 1919–1939* (London: Allen and Unwin: 1949; 6th edition 1963), pp. 74–5. Recent statistical estimates have suggested that whereas real wage growth did not decline by as much as previously thought, there was nonetheless a significant slow down in the 1900s, C.H. Feinstein, 'What really happened to real wages', *Economic History Review*, Vol. XLIII (1989), pp. 351–2.

40 'All records broken: Unprecedented profits', was the headline of the review of 1907, *Oldham Chronicle*, 28 December 1907.

41 A. Fowler and T. Wyke, *The Barefoot Aristocrats: A History of the Amalgamated Association of Operative Cotton Spinners* (Littleborough: George Kelsall: 1987); W. Lazonick, 'Industrial relations and technical change: the case of the self acting mule', *Cambridge Journal of Economics*, Vol. 3 (1979), pp. 231–262.

42 J.H. Clapham, *An Economic History of Modern Britain; Machines and National Rivalries* (Cambridge, Cambridge University Press: 1951), p. 322.

43 Feinstein, 'What really happened to real wages?', p. 339.

44 *Textile Mercury*, 15 April and 2 November 1895.

45 J. Porter, 'Industrial Peace in the Cotton Trade 1875–1913', *Yorkshire Bulletin of Economic and Social Research*, 19, May (1967), pp. 49–59.

46 *Board of Trade Report on Wages*, q. 7567.

47 'Cotton trade wages', *Oldham Chronicle*, 4 July 1908.

48 Toms, thesis, ch. 6.

49 Burgess, *The Origins of British Industrial Relations*, p. 232.
50 Joyce, *Work, Society and Politics*, pp. 339–40.
51 V. Lenin, *Imperialism: The Highest Stage of Capitalism* (London, Lawrence and Wishart: 1933); as an example of 'reformism', Mawdsley, the spinners' union leader was a Conservative party supporter. As a mouthpiece of the senior minders, the *Cotton Factory Times* represented the views of moderate trade unionism; Burgess, *The Origins of British Industrial Relations*, p. 249.
52 Burgess, *Origins of British Industrial Relations*, p. 248.
53 C. Macara, *Recollections by Charles Macara* (London, Cassell: 1922).
54 Although the formal Brooklands agreement broke down in 1905 (Turner, *Trade Union Growth*, p.) the spirit of the system remained in place, Porter, 'Industrial peace', pp. 49–61.
55 J. White, Lancashire Cotton Textiles, in C. Wrigley (ed.), *A History of British Industrial Relations* (Brighton: Harvester Press: 1982), pp. 222–5.
56 Lazonick, 'Industrial Relations', p. 254.
57 Toms, thesis, pp. 347 and 406.
58 Defined here as the difference between the sales value of output and all non capital and labour based costs.
59 The companies for which such data was available for the years between these dates were Osborne, Eccles, Sun Mill, Werneth, and Whiteley; see Toms, thesis, table 1.2, p. 28, for source documents.
60 Layton, *The Relations of Capital and Labour*, pp. 34–6.
61 Feinstein, 'What really happened to real wages?', p. 347.
62 Feinstein, 'What really happened to real wages?', p. 351; Feinstein's conclusion on cotton rested on the Smith and Horne 'An index number', which only included companies with London quotations. Lancashire companies with local quotations enjoyed more equally if not more spectacular return to profit during the 1900s (see chapter 9, table 9.5).
63 Lazonick and Mass, 'Performance of British Cotton', table 1, p. 6.
64 The number of firms was used as a surrogate for the number of factories; the multi plant firm was a rarity, and even where the owners were the same, new factories were usually floated separately, thereby acquiring the status of an independent firm (see Toms, thesis, especially chapters 8 and 9).
65 This can be confirmed from the detailed figures for spinning presented by Lazonick and Mass, 'The Performance of British Cotton', appendix 1, table A1, p. 40. which show a 10.2% increase (output per operative, 1904, 7316 lbs; 1907, 8061 lbs) during the upswing years of 1904–7 on the basis of their single year output data and 5.3% increase (output per operative, 1904, 7220 lbs; 1907, 7604 lbs) when calculated on the basis of three year average output.
66 According to the detailed data in Lazonick and Mass, 'The Performance of British Cotton', appendix 1, table A1, p. 40. productivity increased by 4% between 1901 and 1912. Using the same data, a decline of 1.51% can be shown to have occurred in output per operative for the period 1901–13 (table 8, p. 21). Conclusions depend heavily on the years selected for measurement.
67 Sandberg, *Lancashire in Decline*, p. 97.
68 Chapman, *The Lancashire Cotton Industry*, p. 158.
69 Lazonick, 'Industrial Relations', pp. 253–7; Lazonick, 'Production Relations', p. 505.
70 *Rochdale Observer*, 4 January 1890, p. 6; *Textile Mercury*, 5 December 1896.
71 Joyce, *Work, Society and Politics*, pp. 339–40.

72 *Rochdale Observer*, 13 April 1892. All the mills of the town, with one exception, were closed on the morning of James Heap's funeral in 1892, and flags flew at half mast above the mills, the school, the educational institute, and the Conservative club, each symbolising a locus of power and influence for the departed industrialist and his successors. Most of the local population appeared to turn out to pay their respects.

73 *Rochdale Observer*, 9 April 1892.

74 J. S. Toms, 'Growth Profits and Technological Choice: The Case of the Lancashire Cotton Textile Industry', *Journal of Industrial History*, Vol. 1 (1998), p. 42, compares wages per hand and spindles per hand for the four ring companies then in existence, the three Milnrow companies and Palm mill of Oldham with four Oldham mule companies.

75 Winterbottom, *Cotton spinning calculations*, p. 261. Jewkes and Gray, *Wages and labour*, p. 129.

76 Production at the throstle section of the Fielden spinning plant at Waterside was facilitated by an 'army of doffers', *Todmorden Advertiser*, 9 November 1889, p. 4.

77 According to the recollections of former ring spinners; Kenney, *Cotton Everywhere*, pp. 130–1.

78 Merrtens, 'The hours and cost of labour', p. 160; the mill at Roubaix had 13.3 operatives per 1000 spindles. The comparable figure for mule spinning was 4.86, or 206 spindles per operative (Wood, 'Factory Legislation', p. 316).

79 Toms, thesis, p. 98.

80 See above and the commentary in the *Rochdale Observer*, 13 April 1892.

81 *Oldham Chronicle*, 29 June 1912; Porter, 'Industrial peace' p. 55; Jewkes and Gray, *Wages and labour*, Ch. 9.

82 Fowler and Wyke, *The Barefoot Aristocrats*.

83 Burgess, *The Origins of British Industrial Relations*, p. 239.

84 Wood, 'Statistics of wages', pp. 134–7.

85 For example in the debate between Sandberg and Lazonick; the data in Lazonick, 'Factor costs', appendices 1 and 2, was derived from Winterbottom, *Cotton spinning calculations*, although that source contained no supporting breakdown of its departmental labour cost statistics, pp. 272–3.

86 Winterbottom, *Cotton spinning calculations*, pp. 212–3.

87 Toms, 'Growth, Profits and Technological Choice'; material costs averaged 70.9% and 74.7% of total costs respectively for samples comparable ring and mule companies.

88 Table 5.3. The tendency was for ring mills to be in the high 60%s and mule mills to be in the low 70%s.

89 The Osborne produced 32s/50s warp and 40s/70s weft; Worrall, *Cotton spinners and manufacturers' directory*, 1890.

90 BPP, *Board of trade report*, C.7567.

91 The flexibility of vertical specialisation and its advantages were noted in Jewkes, 'Is British Industry Inefficient?' pp. 9–10.

92 Lazonick, 'The Cotton Industry', pp. 21–2.

93 Blaug, 'The productivity of capital', appendix C, p. 379.

94 Burgess, *The origins of British industrial relations*, p. 232.

Index

For Product Safety Concerns and Information please contact our EU
representative GPSR@taylorandfrancis.com
Taylor & Francis Verlag GmbH, Kaufingerstraße 24, 80331 München, Germany

www.ingramcontent.com/pod-product-compliance
Lightning Source LLC
Chambersburg PA
CBHW061836220326
41599CB00027B/5303